What You Need To Know About...
MASONS

ED DECKER

HARVEST HOUSE PUBLISHERS
Eugene, Oregon 97402

Scripture quotations are from the King James Version of the Bible.

WHAT YOU NEED TO KNOW ABOUT MASONS

Copyright © 1992 by Harvest House Publishers
Eugene, Oregon 97402

Library of Congress Cataloging-in-Publication Data

Decker, Ed.
    What you need to know about Masons / Ed Decker.
    ISBN 0-89081-945-9
    I. Title.
  PS3552.E253W48   1992
  813'.54—dc20   91-37788
                                                                     CIP

Printed in the United States of America.

Foreword

When I began to study Freemasonry with a critical eye, it meant that I had to look back at my own father and grandfather, as well as their fathers before them for almost 200 years. They were honest men, church men who took our faith, our family, and our country seriously, fighting in its many wars. Generation after generation, each son followed after his father and entered into membership in the Lodge. That line ended when I stepped out of the DeMoLay to join the Mormon Church.

The Mormon Church told me that Masonry was a society of "secret combinations" and "works of darkness." I was forbidden to continue membership in the DeMoLay, and later, as an active Mormon, I would *not* seek to follow my father into the Lodge. Years later, after I became a born-again Christian, while I was at a service in a Baptist church teaching on the LDS Temple ritual, I discovered from an angry church deacon that the ritual of the Masonic Lodge was the actual foundation of the LDS Temple ritual. I knew that if what he said was true, I would have to expose the roots of Masonry to the same light of truth that I was bringing to bear on Mormonism. That was easier said than done.

When one goes out to investigate a secret society, there are certain things you discover immediately. First, there is precious little original or first-source material available, and second, you mustn't believe much of what you do find.

I found that while there were many articles available extolling the virtues and good works of the Masonic fraternities, they revealed virtually *nothing* that would give me the first inkling of the actual working of the Lodge, and vehemently denied any religious undertones to their activities.

I went to the Seattle Public Library and found numerous titles on microfilm. However, when I went to the shelves, I discovered that every title that promised information of an internal nature was missing. Several books were listed in a special collections section where the books could not be checked out. The reader must use such books under a controlled environment. However, much to the amazement of the librarian, but adding to my own growing suspicions, those few books were nowhere to be found; they had just disappeared. I soon discovered that the Seattle Library was not alone in this regard. Someone was systematically removing *all* sensitive material from public access, on a national basis. The results were the same at *every* public library in *every* city I visited over the next ten years.

I began to frequent several used-book stores, where I knew the owners picked up books from estate sales. It was reasonable to believe that some of these elderly men whose libraries would be acquired in this manner would have belonged to the Lodge and would have some of the esoteric books I sought. I hit pay dirt. However, I had to visit quite regularly, since once the books made it to the shelves, they would be quickly reclaimed by the Lodge, at whatever price was asked.

I stumbled onto several private Masonic libraries, met a few former Masons who gave me their own small collections, and was able to make just one wonderfully large purchase through a Masonic Fraternity supply house. My library expanded to hundreds of key volumes and thousands of articles and pieces of Masonic paraphernalia. The job was no longer one of searching for material, but one of absorbing the complex inner workings of the craft.

At the same time, I went through a similar review of Christian material pertaining to the Lodge, and with just a few key exceptions I found the church woefully unprepared to deal with the subject. I also didn't understand the absolute pain and anguish through which this book would be birthed. I'm not counting the death threats and several attempts I have personally experienced while researching the book. I'm speaking of the thousands of hours of reading, the thousands of interviews, the hundreds of public meetings and confrontations. I'm speaking of the hundred different times I have been forced back into my research as the Holy Spirit has shown me that I had still more to learn, more to unearth.

Little did I realize that as I did this, the book I planned to write and the one the Holy Spirit wanted me to write would be two entirely different works. I finally decided to follow the prompting of the Holy Spirit.

After all these years of intense research and study, the great exposé of Freemasonry that I had planned to write still lies within all those esoteric Lodge Books, Monitors, Guides, and Manuals I have read and stored on my library shelves. It remains in the hundreds of file folders where data I have gathered in every kind of form is crammed into several four-drawer legal file cabinets.

I became sidetracked from that monumental endeavor as I became more immersed in the fruits of the system rather than continuing in its study. In these ten years or so I have become significantly involved in many hundreds of individual lives, families, and churches severely damaged or destroyed in that process of "good men becoming better," and the experience has established a far different perspective in my heart.

This book is a novel. However, its story is a composite of some of the many real-life stories in which I have been a participant. (The names have been changed to protect the privacy of the individuals involved.) The town of Badger Lake is my own invention. The State of Montana was chosen because no part of this story took place there and because I love the Gold West Country around Dillon, where I placed the town.

When any character in the novel is speaking on behalf of the Freemasonic fraternity, I have tried to make his words and tone realistically match those I read of real Masons giving real testimonies either in person or in actual Masonic magazines and periodicals. In several cases, I have used mixed fragments of actual statements with some literary license. I wanted every one of those statements to be as authentic as possible. In one case I mention a senator, the Governor, and the Lieutenant Governor of Montana attending a meeting as Masonic brothers.

That is historic fact, and came from a Masonic news story published in the August 1990 *Scottish Rite Journal*.

In reciting actual Ritual content and action, I have again drawn from several sources. The Lodges in each State or Grand Lodge jurisdiction usually differ in a modest degree when it comes to such things. I therefore used as my base and standard the 1974 edition of *Duncan's Masonic Ritual and Monitor*, which is the official Freemason's guide to the Symbolic Degrees. However, I again mixed in certain variations which I took from the official Monitors from the Grand Lodges of the States of Washington, Nevada, Georgia, and Arkansas. The material on Job's Daughters came from the 1975 *Ritual and Monitor*, published by the Supreme Guardian Council of the Order, as well as several *Masonic News* articles.

The material on the funeral came from my own personal experience in attending the funeral of a dear friend who was also a Mason, plus the official *Masonic Burial Service Ritual*, by Robert Macoy, published in 1983. The material on the initiation of the Royal Ambassadors came from the manual entitled *Royal Ambassador Ceremonies/Dramas and Recognitions*, published by the Brotherhood Commission of the Southern Baptist Convention, 1988. While it is my intent in the story to show the disturbing parallels between the Masonic rituals of initiation and some of the Royal Ambassador initiations, *it is not my position that the Royal Ambassadors are in any way any formal part of Freemasonry.*

I am telling you all this up front because I want you to know that I am writing with authenticity and scholarship, and also that this is supposed to be a work of fiction, which you need to just sit back and enjoy reading that way, without flipping pages back and forth checking for footnotes.

Throughout the story I have struggled to keep my finger on the root problem in Freemasonry, which is that it truly is a form of religion that has its own creed, religious instruction, and ritual that is Universalist in nature and must surely separate its real Christian members from full service to Christ. When a father and a husband bows his knee at an altar where Baal and Zoroaster have equal recognition and power as the God of Abraham, Isaac, and Jacob, in a Lodge where the precious name of Jesus is specifically removed so as not to offend, that father and husband has bowed his knee to Baal, and his family and his church will reap the fruit of that submission.

Herein lies the matter of the Lodge. It is spiritually alarming that the sins of the fathers have left a door open to the adversary in the lives of Masonic families and in churches where Masons are in leadership. *Those doors can and must be closed forever.* I pray that this novel will give the reader the insight, direction, and motivation to take whatever personal action is needed.

—*Ed Decker*

Introduction

When the average American thinks of the Masonic Lodge, the thoughts are often of children's burn centers, hospitals, and the Shrine Circus, where handicapped children are often carried to the front-row seats in the strong arms of weeping men who are wearing the red fezzes of their fraternity.

Rarely do we see a parade without these same Shriners driving up and down the parade route in their little cars and motorcycles, wearing clothes out of the Arabian nights, bringing laughter to the little children lined up along the sidewalks.

On an occasion of poor timing years back, I had the occasion to have booked a room in the same hotel where a national Shriners convention was being held and had a sleepless night as these men seemed to bounce off the walls of the hallways enjoying their night of relentless fun.

On more serious occasions, such as the laying of public building cornerstones or at the funeral service of a Lodge member, these same men, dressed in somber attire, wearing their ornate sashes and brass-medallioned chains of office and ceremonial aprons, will perform with solemn dignity the rites handed down through centuries of ritual secrecy.

The Freemasonic Lodges are often thought of as a dying breed of fraternal and social groups that sprang into existence to feed the needs of a rural and early industrial America. "Live and let live," I am told. "These are just some old people living out the

9

past with pomp and ceremony." The *Seattle Times*, in a special October 1982 report that gave credence to this thought, said that the average age of a man joining the Lodge is 38. It reported that the great growth of Freemasonry during and after World War II has meant that now its members are dying off. In 1981 just over 1200 new members were inducted in Washington, but 1536 Masons died.

Today much effort is being spent at the national, state, and local levels to create ways to make Freemasonry more acceptable and desirable to the general public so that this trend can be reversed. The experts are trying to bring the Craft public with a "happy face."

Yet once you get past the good-old-boy fraternal side of the Craft, the funny hats and slippers of the Shriners, and the sheltered reputation of the local Blue Lodge Masonic groups, there is something beyond the colorful mask—an aura of mystery, power, and intrigue, complete with undertones of conspiracy and backroom politics.

As ever-present as Masonry hangs on the edge of the public eye, we see it even more subtly present in the Christian community. Except for the ritual funeral service for the Masonic dead, and an occasional march from the Lodge to a selected church for services, the Lodge leaves it to the individual member to select and attend the church of his choice.

On the other end of that spectrum, however, is the church on whose board sits a majority from the Lodge, or whose deacons or elders share Lodge secrets that are in keeping with their higher allegiance to the Lodge, sworn by blood oath, an aloofness from the rest of the church body. These are "good men" who attend regularly and are often the financial backbone of many small congregations.

One pastor shared with me his frustration with Freemasonry in his small, rural church. He put it this way: "As faithful as these men are, I always feel at board meetings that there is a second agenda which is not open to me. It's like they get their marching orders from the Lodge on how to conduct the business of the church. They are good men, but they seem to operate with some higher knowledge than the rest of us. There is no submission to the authority of the church and its other members. It's like their church involvement is just another part of that hidden second agenda."

On closer inspection, there has been something else different about these men. The factory worker in the plant would never dare to greet the owner on the assembly line, but in the work of the Lodge that same man would proudly stand elbow-to-elbow with the factory owner himself. Bank president, grocer, or farmer, all bow together in submission to the Worshipful Master of the Lodge. President, senator, and federal judge could walk arm-in-arm with the blue collar workers of America! Masonry seemed to be the answer to the American dream.

It was upon this platform that Masonry grew in the early nineteenth century. Already having taken root from French and English Masonry (and a definite factor in the radical steps of tearing Colonial America away from English rule), the superstructure had already been built in the late eighteenth century. Masonry was an American kind of organization. It was a "cross your heart and hope to die" kind of group where you could trust the guy next to you with your life and where every member swore an oath to do just that.

Where did the Masons actually come from and what are their secrets all about? The order has claimed descent from the builders of the Egyptian pyramids and the temple of Solomon, and most assuredly it claims descent from the stonecutters and artists who built the grand cathedrals of Europe.

The Masons teach that these men were required to learn certain hand signs and grips to identify their level of trade skill as they traveled from country to country working their trade. The trade group eventually became a fraternity and its secrets those of the trade. Eventually nontradesmen were allowed the privilege of fellowship, thereby creating both Operative and Speculative divisions of the symbolic degrees of Masonry. Today the usual title in the local Lodges is that of Free and Accepted Masons.

It was in 1717 that the First Masonic Grand Lodge was formed in London. It is obvious that there were loosely connected Lodges prior to that time for them to even have had the reason to form such an organizational unit. Not much hard evidence exists, however, that gives any credence to modern Masonry's claim for an organizational lineage that goes back much further.

Freemasonry came to the United States while it was still a territory of the Crown. Masonic history gives great detail to its involvement in the making of America. The colonies' movers and pushers were most often found within the fraternity. In his early years Benedict Arnold was a welcome visitor at any Lodge, but after he became America's most notorious traitor, his name was obliterated from Lodge records.

In 1754 a congress of the colonies was held in Albany, New York. Benjamin Franklin, a member and a Freemason, introduced a plan for a perpetual Union of the colonies, and on July 4, 1754, his proposal failed by only one vote of being ratified by the colonies.

One great event that fired the imagination of the American zealots and hastened the Revolution was the Boston Tea Party. Three British ships lay in that harbor laden with tea. On the night of December 13, 1773, at a large Masonic meeting, it was decided that the tea should not be landed. When the decision was announced, Samuel Adams, the great patriot, arose and gave the *word*. That *word* was answered from outside with a war whoop, and at a signal from John Hancock (a Mason), Paul Revere (also a Mason), and a questionable band of Indians, *the members of the Boston Masonic Lodge* left the tavern in which they met and cast the tea overboard.

On April 18, 1775, British troops were sent to arrest Samuel Adams and John Hancock for treason. Joseph Warren, a Mason, rang the alarm bells of Boston, and Paul Revere, a Mason, rode to Lexington and fame and called the Minutemen to arms—and thus began the Revolutionary War.

On April 19, 1783, eight years to the day after the war began, George Washington, a Mason, proclaimed that the war was ended, and a treaty of peace was signed. The Revolution was fought and won under the First Continental Congress, with Peyton Randolph, a Mason, at its head. John Hancock, a Mason, was President of the Second and Third Congresses. The Third Congress, almost all Masons, adopted the Declaration of Independence.

And that Declaration was written upon a white Lambskin, a Mason's Apron. Thomas Jefferson, a deist and a Mason, was a member of that Continental Congress and was the Chairman of the committee that wrote and presented the Declaration of Independence.

In every corner of American history the Masons were present. We recently celebrated the hundredth-year birthday of the greatest modern statue on earth, the Statue of Liberty, a supposed gift of the French to commemorate the Franco-American union. I noticed an intense effort on the part of the Masons to raise funds for its restoration. In checking further, I discovered that its sculptor was the French Freemason, Frederic A. Bartoldi. It was financed through Masonic efforts and dedicated by the Paris Lodge, Alsace-Lorraine, Bartoldi's home Lodge, a gift from the French Masons to their American brothers. It was received and its cornerstone laid on August 5, 1884, by the Grand Lodge of New York, which Lodge also recently rededicated the restored Lady of the Harbor.

A curious piece of the Masonic conspiracy puzzle in the founding of America is the actual street layout for our capital city, Washington D.C. Actually, it's more the *audacity* of the thing rather than the conspiratorial nature of it. You see, the city was laid out in the form of the central Masonic symbols: the Square, the Compass, and the Rule. Winding about the streets of D.C. are a hundred such applications of the Masonic symbols. They are there by design, and I can barely touch the simplest.

Take any good street map of downtown Washington D.C. and find the Capitol Building. Facing the Capitol from the Mall and using the Capitol as the head or top of the Compass, the left leg is represented by Pennsylvania Avenue and the right leg by Maryland Avenue. The Square is found in the usual Masonic position with the intersection of Canal Street and Louisiana Avenue.

The left leg of the Compass stands on the White House and the right leg stands on the Jefferson Memorial. The circle drive and short streets behind the Capitol complete the picture to form the head and ears of what Satanists call the Goat of Mendes or Goat's head.

On top of the White House is an inverted five-pointed star, or pentagram, which is one of the highest-level symbols of witchcraft and Satanism. *The point rests squarely on the White House* and is facing south in true occult fashion. It sits within the intersections of Connecticut and Vermont Avenues, north to Dupont and Logan Circles, with Rhode Island and Massachusetts going to Washington Circle to the west and Mount Vernon Square on the east.

The center of the pentagram is 16th Street where, 13 blocks due north of the very center of the White House, the Masonic *House of the Temple* sits at the top of this occult iceberg.

The Washington Monument stands in perfect line to the intersecting point of the form of the Masonic Square, stretching from the House of the Temple to the Capitol building. Within the hypotenuse of that right triangle sit many of the headquarter buildings for the most powerful departments of government, such as the Justice Department, the U.S. Senate, and the Internal Revenue Service.

It would be great to know that our Capital city is bathed in continual prayer and to believe that its buildings and monuments had been dedicated in prayer, but do you realize that most federal buildings, from the White House to the Capitol Building, have had a cornerstone laid in a Masonic ritual and had specific Masonic paraphernalia placed in each one?

The cornerstones of these buildings contain Masonic documents showing that these buildings have been dedicated to the god of Masonry, Jah-Bul-On.

Freemasonry soon exploded across young, vulnerable America. With the population growing rapidly and our culture still town- or neighborhood-oriented, Lodges popped up in even the smallest villages. The Eastern Star and other women's and youth groups kept pace at its side. However, one event all but ground the racing giant to dust. Captain William Morgan, a resident of Batavia, New York, and a repentant 30-year member of the fraternity, published an exposé of Masonry in 1827 entitled *Illustrations of Masonry*. That in itself was a significantly accurate and brave effort. However, Morgan was kidnapped and killed. His body was never discovered, and his wife and children sank into deep grief. The media played the whole story out for months, and the resultant furor brought a wave of anti-Masonic action that emptied all but the strongest Lodges.

By the mid-nineteenth century, memories faded and the cultural aspects of Lodge life brought memberships back up. With the burst of new industries, America wanted the pomp and ceremony that brushed away the aches of long days and little entertainment. It was here that the Masons moved casually and quietly into the mainstream Christian organizations and churches. With Masons in the White House, Cabinet, Congress, and the Senate, having some of the powerful Masons in the church was an advantage, or so it seemed.

With the Great Depression, the two world wars, and the quantum leap into the new high-tech society of today, the Freemasons look a bit quaint. Yet their power base has enlarged greatly. In the late eighties we had the sixteenth Masonic President, Ronald Reagan, 60 members of the House of Representatives, 18 Senators, 41 members of the Federal Judiciary, and about half the membership in the Judiciary Committee. That is hardly quaint or insignificant. To the pagan much of this will not matter, but to the Christian church in which the Craft is now operating, it should be deeply disturbing. Nothing should separate us from our first love, the

Lord Jesus Christ, that name above all names and the one name that cannot be lawfully uttered in testimony or prayer in virtually any Masonic Lodge.

As Christians we have the *obligation* to look into the corners of our lives to see where the Spirit of God must work, submitting ourselves to His mercy. Herein lies the matter of the Lodge. Put aside fear and study the matter prayerfully!

> Therefore, brethren, we are debtors, not to the flesh, to live after the flesh. For if ye live after the flesh, ye shall die; but if ye through the Spirit do mortify the deeds of the body, ye shall live. For as many as are led by the Spirit of God, they are the sons of God. For ye have not received the spirit of bondage again to fear, but ye have received the Spirit of adoption, whereby we cry, "Abba, Father." The Spirit itself beareth witness with our spirit, that we are the children of God (Romans 8:12-16).

Chapter
1

Jennifer Moore ran across the expanse of lawn, looking up as the students poured from the building, her eyes searching the crowd expectantly. She was out of breath with the excitement of her announcement and the effort of jogging the dozen or so blocks from the apartment to the campus, trying to catch Jeff before he was swept away in the noon-hour rush.

She caught the glimpse of his blond head and broad shoulders towering above the rest as he stood on the stairs, leaning down to listen as some young man shared a special word. Jeff was grinning widely and she knew he was enjoying the moment, fully absorbed in watching the fellow's face as he nodded his open approval of whatever it was he was hearing.

———◆———

She thought back to the day over four years ago when she first saw Jeff in the university bookstore. She was working at the register when he dropped a load of books on the counter. Jennifer looked up into that broadly smiling face and deep eyes so intense that she felt as though they were on fire. She fell instantly in love and turned a deep crimson red because she was sure that this giant of a man could read every thought in her suddenly addled mind.

She was almost incapable of ringing up the sale, unable to keep from looking back into his eyes every few seconds, as though she was afraid he would vanish if she looked at the register for more than an instant at a time. It seemed that he just stood there in the center of some golden haze, grinning from ear to ear while she beat undecipherable numbers into the register in some sort of panic, trying to complete the transaction before she passed out from her failure to breathe during the eternity of the last several minutes. She prayed for some miracle to happen that would allow her to see this man again, that he would not just walk out of her life right there in the bookstore.

The miracle occurred when he wrote out a check and laid it down with his student ID card. She stared at them. There was no other name on the check! He was single and his ID said that he was a junior! Jennifer wrote out his student number on the back of the check and actually breathed for the first time. Jennifer handed the card back to him with a victorious smile. She had his name, his dorm address, *and* his phone number.

CHAPTER ONE

"Thank you, Mr. Moore! Please come in again," she said as she pushed the package across the counter.

As Jeff reached for the books, his hand brushed hers for just an instant. Their eyes locked and this time they both blushed. It would be months later before she found out that Jeff Moore was having similar problems of his own that day.

Jennifer smiled as she recalled the urgency with which she pursued Jeff Moore and the satisfaction she felt that night they first professed their love to each other.

The summer after Jeff graduated, they traveled to her home in Badger Lake, Montana, where they were married in the little Baptist church that had been her church home since she was a child. It was a month of sparkling fun—attending bridal showers, planning the wedding, and organizing the reception at the Masonic Hall.

Every family member and friend since grade school had the chance to check over this young minister she was marrying, and every girl's head turned as she guided Jeff arm-in-arm through the town. Within it all was the special joy and knowledge that the Lord had brought them together for His purpose, that they were one in Christ, that Jeff made her feel loved and secure throughout her entire being.

If their Montana trip was the icing on the wedding cake, the two weeks that they spent with Jeff's folks in California was the meat and potatoes of life. Jeff's dad was the pastor of a growing church in San Diego. His mother and father just encompassed her with real love and tenderness. Jeff shared from the pulpit at his home church the Sunday they arrived, and the church

members almost smothered her before Jeff could res-
cue her that morning.

She remembered watching with some satisfaction
as Jeff and his dad took time each day to quietly talk in
the study. She knew that the foundation from which
her husband grew was a solid one.

It seemed like only days before they had to return to
school, loaded down with all the gifts they had collected. She still had one year to go, and they had both
agreed that Jeff needed to complete a master's degree
if he were to make the ministry his life's work. Now it
was almost over. Not only was Jeff completing his
master's degree, but he had been working as a teaching assistant during his off hours.

———◆———

Jennifer waved frantically as Jeff turned his eyes her
way, and she felt that rush of joy as his face lit up in
recognition. He pointed toward her as he spoke to the
student at his side and quickly came her way.

"Jenny," he smiled broadly, "can you catch lunch
with me? I don't have to be back until 2:30!" Jeff
caught her up in his arms and gave her a giant hug.

"Not only will I have lunch with you, *Mister* Moore,
but I'll even buy today. I've got some great news and
you are just not going to believe it!" She held out an
envelope, waving it in front of him.

"The pulpit committee from Badger Lake Baptist
Church wants to know if you would be interested in
interviewing for the pastorate there. Pastor Taylor has

been there for over 30 years and is retiring this summer," she said, opening the letter for Jeff to see.

"They'll pay for our airfare there and back for you to interview and preach for a couple of services, right after school. We can stay with mom and dad! At least we'll get a trip back home for a few weeks . . . and maybe a senior pastor's calling," she continued happily as they walked into the Student Union building.

They worked their way through the students into the staff lunchroom and didn't talk until they brought their food trays to a quiet table. After a short grace, Jeff squeezed her hand and reached for the letter.

He silently read through the letter and looked up at his watchful wife. "It's quite an opportunity, Jen. There are over 150 people at Badger Lake. It's not like working through five or six years as an associate. I wonder how much your dad had to do with this?"

Jennifer laughed. "I bet he's on the pulpit committee! I just can't believe that Pastor Taylor is leaving. He baptized me a hundred years ago at the lake, way before the baptistry was even built."

"Well, before I head back to classes today, we can give your folks a call and make arrangements. *Talk about timing!* I'll be finished here next Friday and we can leave right away. I wonder how many other candidates they'll interview," Jeff mused as he reached over and speared a tomato from his wife's salad.

———◆———

Jeff scanned the mountain terrain below intently as the Delta jet banked over the Silver Bow mountains and headed into Butte, crossing Pipestone Pass as it lined up for descent into the airport.

"I'll bet there are twice as many people in San Diego as in this whole state," he announced to his wife. "I wonder what it holds for us, Jenny?" he asked almost whimsically.

"Well," she responded, "I love this place almost as much as I love you, Jeff. Whatever it has for us, I'm sure it will be *exactly* what the Lord wants for us. It may just be the place where we start our own life, our own family."

Jennifer reached over and gave her husband a quick kiss on the cheek. "Here's a kiss to get you started right," she laughed as the plane touched down.

Jennifer's parents were waiting as they stepped off the plane, and they greeted the pair with great exuberance. Jennifer was their only child, and through the years they had been close to her side in everything she did. When Jenny chose to leave Montana to go to Bible college, it was a rough time for them. On the one hand, they wanted the very best for her, and yet they had always assumed that she would live out her life, if not in Badger Lake itself, at least up to Butte or even Missoula or Great Falls. Little did they expect that she would fall in love with someone from California! They were pretty nervous people until they could see for themselves what kind of son-in-law she brought them.

For once the bags were on the luggage belt by the time they reached the baggage claim area, and they were soon turning south on the Interstate heading toward Dillon and Badger Lake. Her mother made much ado at seating Jeff in the front seat of a brand-new Lincoln Town Car, while Jennifer exclaimed over the prize.

"Your dad is now traveling all over the state with his Lodge work," her mother explained. "He just wore out that Ford and I told him that if he was going to be so important, he ought to drive a car to match."

Roy Wallace was a quiet man with little to say. What he did say, and often, was that his wife, Ruth, said enough for them both, and then some. What he did with great regularity, however, was to methodically nod as though in agreement with some silent conversation he was having with himself. As Jeff looked over at his father-in-law, Roy was smiling and nodding with great vigor.

Jeff looked out at the mountains as the car powered its way up Deer Lodge Pass. There is such beauty here that it overwhelms you, he thought. He listened with half an ear to his mother-in-law as she updated Jennifer on all the local gossip, and then he let his thoughts drift back to the scenery again.

Roy Wallace cleared his throat and sighed. "It's going to be just wonderful having you two so close, Jeff. Ruth and I want you to know how proud we are to have you for our son-in-law."

"Hang on there, Roy. I've got a pulpit committee to convince yet, but it's pretty exciting to even be in the running," Jeff responded with his broadest smile.

"Well, you know you have our votes, except it's going to be a little strange calling you Pastor Moore," Roy answered with a short laugh and a few nods. "Win Johnson, the fellow who wrote you, will give you a call in the morning to set up a meeting. You're off the clock until tomorrow."

The evening sped by and Jeff lay in the bed at Jennifer's side long into the night, thinking through the last six years that brought him to this small town in the Montana mountains. School had occupied the last 18 years of his life.

Actually 20 years, if I count preschool and kindergarten, he thought. My whole life has been to prepare me to step out into the world, and here I am stepping out into my in-laws' house. Not too far a leap, but a pretty safe one. I just pray that we are in the Lord's will whatever decisions are made.

Jeff reached out and gently laid his hand on Jennifer's shoulder, then quietly prayed. He smiled in the dark as Jennifer stirred beside him. Jenny's so excited about all this, and I am too, I guess. He thought about the sermon he would preach on Sunday and envisioned the two of them standing at the back door, shaking hands with the congregation as they left.

———◆———

The brightness of the morning sun had already filled the room when Jeff awoke. Jenny had long since gone down to the kitchen to fix breakfast with her mother. He leaped up as though he were late for class and raced through a quick shower and shave.

"Hi, bright eyes," his wife teased as he came into the kitchen. "Sit down and let me start your engines with a cup of good Montana coffee. Win Johnson has already called and I told him you would be by his hardware store at 11:00. Okay?"

Jeff settled into a chair at the table, grinning back at his wife's contagious smile and reaching gratefully for the proffered mug of steaming coffee. The clock above the sink said it was still only 8:15 in the morning. Jennifer's mother was only an instant behind the coffee with an overflowing plate of bacon and eggs.

"There's buttered toast on the table and the last of the jam I made up last summer," she said. "I put the eggs on when you came out of the bathroom. Dad is already in town," she continued. "He opens the insurance office at 8:30 and likes to get down there for a cup of coffee at the cafe first."

Roy Wallace had been opening his office every morning at 8:30 A.M. for almost 30 years, even though 90 percent of all his business was done at the homes or businesses of his clients. His was the *only* local insurance office, and his files contained the insurance histories of almost every family in and around Badger Lake. Roy took great satisfaction that not one of his clients had ever had to fight for a claim, but that he was always there, ready to help, when any emergency came up.

That morning cup of coffee was another daily ritual for him, and his absence would be the major subject of conversation at the diner on those rare days he would fail to show up. Tiny, the cafe owner, whose name was the antithesis of fact, would call the house to see what emergency could have caused such a radical departure from Roy's schedule.

Tiny and Roy had a solemn routine that required the attention of everyone present each morning. One day, more years ago than anyone could remember, Roy came into the cafe and ordered coffee. When Tiny, engrossed in a conversation, absent-mindedly filled the cup only halfway, Roy snorted loudly, "Do you call this a cup of coffee? Do you actually charge people for this?"

Tiny stopped midway in a sentence and with great equanimity brought the coffeepot back and filled the cup to the exact point just below overflowing. The coffee actually formed a convex bulge above the cup rim. Roy met him eyeball to eyeball and without spilling a drop raised the cup to his lips and drank deeply. Putting the cup down with deliberate emphasis, he announced to the small crowd of onlookers, "Finally, the first honest cup of coffee I've had in this place."

Over the years a lot of coffee had been spilled on the counter by both men, but the victories won in this daily battle were larger than life. For the cafe crowd it didn't matter if Tiny spilled it going in or Roy spilled it going up. Either result brought on a carnival mood that lasted for hours.

———————◆———————

Jeff walked into the hardware store and wandered around the musty old aisles marveling at the ancient wooden shelves and floors, while Win was finishing up mixing a gallon of paint for a customer in the rear. He saw Jeff and called out a greeting. Jeff occupied himself by looking at the wall of fishing and hunting photos behind the register. Badger Lake was one of the best fishing lakes in the state, and over the years it had given up some real trophies, as the hundreds of photos attested.

There was a picture there of Jenny holding up a very large trout with both hands. She was probably ten when the picture was taken. It was quite the event at the time, and over the years she often stopped in to be sure the picture was still there and to remember her great luck that day. It was one of the first things Jennifer had shown Jeff when they came here for the wedding. She told him that someday she was going to show that picture to her own son or daughter.

There was also a picture of Win holding up a string of huge trout that only a strong man could lift. Win was even taller than Jeff, broad-shouldered and rugged. He had been a great football hero in the early 50's and had helped bring Badger Lake High into the state finals his senior year. He played four years at Montana State and was heading for the pros until a crushing knee injury sidelined him in his senior year. He had brought back a tiny cheerleader for a wife and took over the management of the family hardware store for his ailing father.

Win and Sue Johnson had a full house with eight kids, and now there were even a few grandchildren keeping things active. The Johnsons were constantly involved in both school and church activities, and with six large strapping sons they had been the backbone of the high school sports program for quite some time. They had a deep faith and had led many people to the Lord over the years. Win had been on the church board for years, and it was in that capacity that he had assumed the chairmanship of the pulpit committee.

When Win finished with the customer he came over immediately. "It's great to see you again, Jeff," he said, shaking Jeff's hand warmly. "I wanted to talk to you privately before all the recruiting set in. You're quite the popular young minister around these parts, you know," he added with a twinkle in his eye.

"Not bad for a guy who's never been out of school," Jeff retorted. "I'm embarrassed to even be in the running with any real ministers."

"Well, that's one of the things I wanted to talk to you about, Jeff. There aren't any other candidates coming, that is unless *you* don't take the position. I think you're just the kind of pastor we need here in Badger Lake, but I want you to come in here with your eyes wide open."

Win smiled as he noted Jeff's shocked look at his pronouncement. "I'm sorry to be the bearer of such good news, Jeff," he laughed, "but this is a small church in a family-centered town somewhere out in the middle of the Montana sky country. The people here want to be comfortable with everything, including who's preaching to them, marrying their kids, and burying their old folks.

"Dick Taylor has been pastor here since I was a kid in high school," he continued. "No one can really remember the time when he wasn't here for them, and they're nervous about what's going to happen to our church when he's gone. He's a part of our lives. We know that our faith is in Christ, but this man has been a rock for us and his shoes aren't going to be easy to fill."

Win walked to the window and swept his arm across the breadth of his view of the street. "This town has been asleep for a long time, Jeff. We're like some 1950's community frozen in time. We move slow in the things we do here, and decisions like this that involve the lives of hundreds of people operate by a tradition that's hard to define.

"The church *will* embrace you, Jeff, because you're family to us. Your wife grew up here in this town; she went to this school and attended this church. While you represent a trained minister of the gospel with a Master's of Divinity degree, you're married to family, and you're reachable to these ranchers and farmers and merchants. You can become someone they can comfortably call during those tough times they all know they'll have. They watched you two get married right here by their own pastor."

Jeff walked to the window and stood next to him, looking onto the street. He was grateful that this man was talking to him the way he was. He felt the strength and heart of the man, and he saw a person he knew he could trust. "I'm not sure I'm anywhere near the quality of a man to replace someone like Pastor Taylor. He's got such a depth of spiritual maturity that it's beyond scary."

"Talk to me about spiritual maturity 30 years from now," Win laughed broadly. "Right now we need all the youth and vigor that you can generate, Jeff."

Win's smile tightened. "There are some problems, too. The young kids are just not being challenged or developed. They mostly come to church because they're told to come, not because it's where their hearts are centered. They can't relate to an elderly pastor, no matter how mighty and godly a man he is. It's one area of badly needed ministry where your youth and enthusiasm can change a lot of lives for the Lord.

"It's not just theory, Jeff. It's a problem in my own family! I just had a knock-down-drag-out battle with our 14-year-old last Sunday. He informed us that he wasn't going to waste his time or God's time in another single Sunday school class. This is a kid who spent most of his last summer vacation on a missions trip to Mexico. He loves God but is sure having a tough time with church. The Johnsons need you too, Jeff!"

Win walked back to the counter, removing the old work apron and tossing it behind the display case filled with ammunition for the numerous guns on display in the wall racks behind him. "We need to go over to Tiny's and meet Pastor Dick and the others for an early lunch. Roy and a few of the board members will be there with him."

Win started toward the back of the store but suddenly stopped in midstride, causing Jeff to stop quickly only a foot or two from him. Win turned, and with eyes deeply intent on Jeff's he spoke in a solemn tone. "One thing more, Jeff. This church board is composed of a group of men who have an allegiance that goes beyond that to the Lord and this church. They're Masons. I guess I'm the only one who has ever been on the board who isn't one, and that's because I took over my dad's board seat when he died, and he was a Mason. Even then, I'm sure it was expected that I'd join the Lodge right away myself."

"I don't want to have to admit that they really run things, but it's true. They run the town and they run the church. Just understand that there is a level of politics here that no one will ever talk about, but everyone knows is there." Without another word, Win locked up and led Jeff across the parking lot to Tiny's Cafe.

Jeff silently rolled those last comments back through his mind several times as they left the hardware store and walked to the cafe. He knew that Win had given him a piece of information that he considered very important and highly significant. Yet he knew that his wife and in-laws looked at the Masons as something that added to their Christian life and wondered where any conflict could possibly exist. As they stepped into the cafe, he turned his thoughts to the events at hand.

———————— ◆ ————————

As they worked their way to the back of the cafe, past Tiny's warm greeting and the hellos of the customers already settling in for an early lunch, Roy jumped up from the table of men and came toward them with an eager welcome.

"Well, Win, have you checked this guy out for us?" he asked. "I hear he comes with some pretty good recommendations."

"Everything seems okay so far, Roy," Win parried, "except I hear that his father-in-law is a pretty bad character."

Charlie Miller and Steve Hanson rose from their seats across the table, extending their hands in greeting. Both were board members and the other two members of the pulpit committee. Charlie was the manager of the local Grange, the rancher's cooperative that served the area, and also a city councilman of long standing. Steve was a pharmacist who owned and operated the town drugstore, next door to Roy's insurance agency. He also was the leader for the Royal Ambassadors, the church's youth program for boys.

Pastor Taylor stood and warmly greeted them, offering the seat next to him to Jeff. "It's good to see you, Jeff," he smiled. "You're a welcome sight for these old eyes."

Jeff took the offered seat and sat down next to the pastor. Dick Taylor was a lanky man with thick white hair and a deep bass voice, and with what can only be called a handsome profile. Over the years the power of that "preacher's voice" and his penetrating eyes had caused untold numbers of sinners to fall across the steps of the altar in woeful repentance and confession of sin. He walked with a natural stoop, bent in against the pressure of years spent in his battles in a losing war with arthritis. His hands bore the brunt of the worst of the disease. Gnarled and swollen, they were his constant reminders in everything he did that this war had been lost.

CHAPTER ONE

The last winter had been about as bad as it could get. Dick could barely hold his toothbrush in his hand and even had to lay his Bible flat on the pulpit when he preached. At times it took every bit of his determination to just turn the pages. For a man who had spent a lifetime holding his Bible out in his hand like a sword when he spoke, it was almost more than he could bear. He knew it was his last winter in the pulpit.

Once his major passion had been golf, and while he and his wife were retiring to their favorite vacation golf course community in sunny, warm Arizona, he knew that he had waited too long in leaving. There would be no easy days spent on the golf course, enjoying the game with friends in relaxing fellowship. But the pain of the harsh Montana winters would be over, and there was more to do in Arizona than just golf. Once the decision had been made, he could hardly wait to leave. His wife had already gone ahead to begin the process of the move, and he would join her as quickly as he could install Jeff Moore as his replacement.

Dick Taylor watched the young man as he was being greeted by the several other men at the table. He thought back to meeting Jeff for the first time when Jenny had brought him into his study when they had come home for the wedding. The more he watched him during those few weeks, the more he began asking God if this was the one to replace him here at Badger Lake. During this last cold and difficult winter, those prayers became increasingly fervent and took on an urgency that he knew was prompted more by his own personal need for release than by the general needs of his church.

When he felt that this release from ministry had come from the Lord, and was convinced that Jeff Moore was as much God's choice for the pastorate as he was Dick Taylor's choice, he stopped in at the insurance office and shared those thoughts with Roy. Dick reminded him of the conversation they had had when Roy was still so devastated at Jenny's leaving Montana to go away to college.

He had told Roy at the time that even a Baptist minister didn't always know the will of the Lord in every matter, and that they must trust God to protect and guide this young woman whom they both loved so dearly. Now it seemed that the Lord had not only blessed her but had also joined her to a godly man in whom the strong anointing of the Lord was obviously at work.

Roy could hardly disagree with his choice of a replacement, and he sat there listening and nodding along, moist-eyed at the thought of having his only child return to Badger Lake as their pastor's wife. Within minutes the wheels of action were in motion when Win Johnson was called and asked to set up a pulpit committee to begin the process at once. Dick left the office that day confident that he had spent his last winter in Montana.

The fellowship over lunch was warm and light as the men awkwardly poked and prodded around the task of reviewing the man who would most likely be their new pastor. The mood was casual, and before long Dick and Jeff were walking into the church sanctuary, where the pastor was to give Jeff a full tour of the church and parsonage.

Badger Lake Baptist Church was built in 1895. It sat on the southwest corner of what was once the main north/south road through town, at the intersection of the east/west county road that came up from Dillon and ran out to the lake. It eventually joined up (about a hundred meandering miles west of the lake) with the state road up to Darby and Missoula.

When the town and the through traffic grew large enough, the pressure eventually pulled the north/south state road and main business street one block east of the church. In later years the highway came through one mile east of town and brought further isolation to the little town and the first stone church in southwestern Montana.

The original church was still used for worship every week. It was laboriously and beautifully constructed of quarry stone hauled in from the mountains south of there by rail many years earlier. At the time, the Utah and Northern Railroad had trains coming in regularly all the way up from Salt Lake City to the railroad town of Terminus, now the city of Dillon, just a few miles southeast of Badger Lake.

It boasted a beautiful set of stained-glass windows, rare in the early Montana territory and almost nonexistent in most small Baptist churches anywhere. The church was also unique in that it had a three-story belfry with a real working bell that was shipped in all the way from England. It still rang in every New Year and had announced the wedding of every church member for almost one hundred years. In fact, the very last wedding it rang in was that of Jeff and Jenny Moore. Until the Badger Lake Fire Department acquired its own siren in the late 1920's, it also served as the town's fire bell.

While the physical quality of the church might have seemed to an outsider to be a little beyond the realm of such a small town and congregation, the actual major share of the cost of construction came from a wealthy stockman's wife who was bound on making the church where they worshiped match the style and grace of her home church in upstate New York. Some early Baptist sage was wise enough to have put this dear soul in charge of the building committee.

The church property occupied a quarter-block of land, with the actual church building taking up the corner quarter of the lot, sitting on a rise up a sloping, well-groomed lawn. To the side sat the Education and Activities Building, which took up another quarter of the property. It was constructed just ten years earlier to make room for the expanding congregational needs.

Behind the Education Building sat a paved parking lot, which filled up the third quarter of the lot, and behind the church on the street side sat the parsonage, with its own drive and yard. A square, two-story building with a wide front porch across the whole width of the house, it was faced with much of the quarry rock left over from the original church construction and was a fine example of home construction at the turn of the century. Just past the house, a small bridge was cover for a year-round stream that ran past the house and bordered the church property. It still yielded some fine trout for those who cared to stop and throw in a line from time to time. Dick resolved many a spiritual problem sitting on the banks of that stream with a fishing pole in his hand.

On the opposite corner of the intersection sat the square, two-story brick building that housed the Badger Lake Masonic Lodge, and next to that the Badger Lake Volunteer Fire Department facilities, built in the same brick by the same bricklayers. All three properties were contemporary with each other, built on land donated by the same widow in memory of her late husband, who was an avid Mason, Baptist, and member of the town's first volunteer fire department. The gift was given to place the objects of his passions forever in the very center of the town at its central intersection. The dear widow certainly did not foresee the fact that time and population growth would bring it all to just one block off-center!

The two men stood quietly at the back of the church, looking down the aisle between the two long rows of wooden pews to the altar. A ray of light reflected off the pulpit, sent softly by the sun, radiating colors through one of the two stained-glass windows on either side of the cross.

Both men were momentarily lost in their thoughts. To Dick, the lunch and Jeff's presence were instruments in closing out a whole portion of a life that had revolved around this place for 30 precious years.

"How many times have I walked alone through this place with the Lord, knelt at that altar, preached from that pulpit," he spoke softly. "Now it's time to say goodbye."

He turned to Jeff. "I only pray that the Lord bless you and Jenny with the joy and the fruit of ministry that has been ours for all these years, Jeff. This old church has been at the center of my life for more years than you have been alive," he laughed. "I have such a peace leaving it and its people in your hands. I know that you are God's man for this place and this people. I feel God's hand, His timing, and His purpose in this whole thing."

Jeff was too stunned to even speak for a few long moments. He was still inhaling the essence of the sanctuary—its age, its beauty, and the feeling of holiness and peace that pervaded the quiet afternoon.

"Does feeling not worthy matter?" he asked the older man.

"Feeling not worthy is the best place to begin," he answered gently. "For what it's worth, that's how I felt 30 years ago and just how I feel today. Remember that old chorus, 'Worthy, worthy, worthy is the Lamb. . .'? It doesn't say worthy is the Pastor," he smiled.

"Son, I know you're struggling with all this, and there's a lot for you and Jenny to pray about. But I want you to know that you're the man that God laid on my heart to turn this ministry over to, and I'm more convinced of it every moment I spend with you.

"I wanted to have you to myself this afternoon as we walked through the church and parsonage. Somehow I wanted to communicate my deep love

for them to you . . . and my love for this congregation. I was asking God to show me some way I could
pass that on to you. But I knew you already had that
understanding as we stood here just a few minutes
ago. I saw it in your face."

The older man walked a ways down the aisle and
then turned around, waving his uplifted arms to the
rafters above. "Do you have any idea how to shake
the cobwebs from this sleepy old place?" They both
laughed heartily.

───────◆───────

"Jen, it's like nothing I've ever experienced before. One day here and I feel like we're nestled in the
very palm of the Lord's hand," he shared after they
finally made it into bed that night. "How do you
really feel about us taking the pastorate here?"

"I'm so excited I could bust, Jeff," she cried. "Did
you know that Sister Taylor has been spending over
half her time in Arizona? The women's ministries
here are just staggering to stay alive. I bet I had ten
phone calls today from some of the young mothers
who want to get together this week. There is so
much I could do here for the Lord!"

"Sweetheart, let's try to slow down just a bit and
pray a little about what we should do," he replied.
"I think I want to say yes to them tomorrow. But,
first, Pastor Taylor gave me a set of master keys for
the church and parsonage, and I want to walk
through the place with you tomorrow morning—
just the two of us. Okay?"

Jenny smiled, snuggling in close to her husband in response. "I'm so proud of you, Jeff," she whispered softly, "and I'm so very happy tonight."

Chapter
2

The first Sunday after their return with their household belongings was some kind of day. Every person who had ever been even loosely associated with Badger Lake Baptist Church showed up for the morning service. There was standing room only more than 30 minutes before church was even to begin. Every member of the choir was there and every usher on duty. Half the people came to say goodbye to the man who had filled the pulpit there for so long and the other half came to check out this Jeff Moore fellow firsthand.

Sunday school had been even more chaotic. There was such a festive spirit that the teachers were unable to teach the study courses and eventually gave up even trying. Pastor Taylor and his wife spent the time going from class to class, shaking hands and whispering private words of encouragement here and there, saying goodbye to as many people as they could as friends crowded around them. Once the decisions had been made and the details worked out, Dick Taylor insisted that he leave at once and let this young man be the single face of authority without further delay.

Jennifer and a few of her friends were already pumping out coffee and sweet rolls at the kitchen window and Jeff was in the church foyer, listening patiently as several elderly ladies were explaining to him why the church needed cushions on at least some of those terrible old pews. Roy Wallace was seated in his usual end-of-the-pew, center-aisle seat up near the front, smiling broadly and nodding away with great enthusiasm.

The service itself was a blur in time. When Dick Taylor finished his goodbyes, there was not a dry eye in the congregation. Jeff could see the depth of the love these people shared with the man who had been their shepherd for so many years. He introduced Jeff in warm, glowing terms and had Jeff stand at his side as he officially passed the mantle of ministry to him. Dick Taylor introduced him as their new pastor, and it was finally time for Jeff to step up to the pulpit and stand before these people.

Jeff silently looked over the faces of the congregation. Every eye was on him. He saw the eager faces, the waiting ears. Placing his hands on the sides of the pulpit, as though to take strength from it, he began to share from his heart with his congregation.

The summer went by with a double-time cadence. Everything was happening at once. Moving into the huge parsonage, their first real house, was both exciting and frustrating for them. Jennifer and her mother and friends spent hour after hour walking through the rooms talking about colors, paints, wallpapers, curtains, and pillows.

The results of the many trips to Dillon and up to Butte began to slowly change the look of the house. Jeff would often walk back to the house from his office to a weary, paint-covered wife who would race to the door, beaming over her latest accomplishment—or who could just as easily begin crying over some event of the day.

Jeff enjoyed the yardwork and found it quite satisfying to ride the lawn tractor, mowing not only their own lawn but also that of the church ground and the edges of the parking areas. Often during these times he worked over his sermons, preaching them out boldly under the din of the engine noise, rehearsing some special phrase over and over again until he was sure it was the best it could be.

Early each morning Jeff would jog north along the full length of Old Main Street, several miles through town, until it joined with the four-lane. Then he would jog back again along the newer road as it returned through the main business street of Badger Lake. At Tiny's Cafe he would cut off the street and into the restaurant, rarely making it to the counter before Tiny would have his hot cup of black coffee waiting for him.

Some of the ranchers and businessmen would be there filling thermoses and enjoying some robust fellowship over coffee. These were special times for Jeff and important in his mind toward becoming established among the townsmen. He fit in easily, a welcome addition to their lives. Jeff was usually back at home before his father-in-law arrived for his normal morning visit to the cafe, but on those days when he might linger over an extra cup, he would take the time to sit down with Roy and chat. Most often their conversations centered around Jenny's latest project at the parsonage or Jeff's activities at the church.

Summer was a busy time for Roy Wallace and his Masonic duties. He was out of town several times each week traveling to affairs around the state or to meetings of the state organizational group, the Grand Lodge, in which he was an officer. While it occupied a great deal of his time, Roy was reluctant to talk much about it to Jeff, except in most general terms.

Roy was in charge of the Lodge's Fourth of July Parade float this year, and had asked Jeff's permission to allow the men to work on its construction in the church parking lot, where there was ample room, and besides, "It was always built there before."

This morning, as Jeff stepped into Tiny's, he noticed that Roy's white Town Car was already in front. Roy was having an early breakfast with Charlie Miller and Steve Hanson. By their formal dress it was obvious that they were on their way out of town on Masonic Lodge business somewhere. Roy looked up and waved Jeff to their table, pushing over some business material to make room for his son-in-law.

"Sit down, Jeff," he said with a great deal of gusto. "It's not often I beat you to Tiny's these days. We're just catching a quick breakfast before we head up to Butte and then over to Billings for a Masonic Reunion tonight. Big doings! Senator Burns is the guest speaker. The Governor and the Lieutenant Governor will be there, too. They're all three Masons, you know," he said with much emphasis.

Jeff took the offered cup of coffee from the ever-faithful Tiny and sat down next to his wife's father. "I can see you're all duded up for something. Jenny mentioned you would be out of town tonight. We were hoping to have you over for dinner before midweek service to check out the new kitchen. Jen just finished redoing it yesterday."

Roy exchanged glances with his two friends and then looked back at his son-in-law. "Jeff," he started, "we were just talking about Jenny. You know, before she left for college, she was quite active in Job's Daughters. In fact, she was the Honored Queen of her Bethel, or chapter, during her senior year of high school."

"I know," responded Jeff. "She mentioned it while she was unpacking some of her plaques and things the other day. She had hauled them over from your attic with a bunch of other boxes, I guess."

Charlie Miller looked up from his plate. "My daughter and her family are moving up to Missoula this month, Jeff. She has been the adult advisor for the Jobies since Jenny was in high school. Roy and I are Executive members of the Bethel Guardian

Council, and we wonder how you would feel if we asked Jenny to take over as their advisor."

Roy interrupted before Jeff could reply. "I know you aren't a Mason and don't understand a whole lot about it, Jeff, but Jenny has been raised in a Masonic family, and as the daughter of a Past Worshipful Master of the sponsoring Lodge and the former Honored Queen of the Bethel, she is the perfect candidate. Besides that, most of the high school girls at church are members, and with Jenny being their advisor, it would tie everything right back through the church. Would you mind if we spoke to her about it?" he asked.

"No, I wouldn't mind at all, Roy," he replied. "It's her choice, really. If Jenny thinks it would help her to encourage these young girls to have a closer walk with the Lord, I'm sure she would be delighted to put some of her energies to work on their behalf. In fact, I'll mention it to her when I get home this morning."

"Well, I'm sure it would help her in her Christian duties just fine," his father-in-law responded with a smile. "As board members at the church, we wouldn't do anything that would be a conflict for either the church or her responsibilities there. Anyway, the Bethel is in recess for the summer, so we have a little time before we have to act," he added. "The Job's Daughters is based on the 42nd chapter, 15th verse of the book of Job. Even the name of their meeting place, Bethel, means Holy Place in the Bible."

CHAPTER TWO

A little later, as Jeff climbed the porch of the house, Jennifer came crashing through the hedges at the side of the house. "Oh, Jeff! Thank the Lord you're home!" she cried with obvious relief. "Please help me, honey," she sobbed as she ran, holding a little wet bundle of limp, damp fur to her. She was still in her nightgown and soaking wet and muddied from head to foot.

Jeff, shocked to see Jennifer in such a state of disarray, quickly jumped from the porch to his wife's side. Reaching into her arms to take the mysterious bundle she held out to him, he was surprised to see that it was a little puppy.

"It was drowning in the creek, Jeff." She was weeping openly now. Her words came between gasps. "I heard it crying from the bedroom window, and when I looked out I saw it trying so frantically to get out of the creek as it was being dragged under. I ran out and jumped in after it. We both nearly drowned, Jeff," she cried out.

Jeff scooped her up in one arm and carried her and the half-drowned dog into the house. "It's going to be all right, honey. It's going to be all right," he assured her as she clung to him, her arms wrapped tightly around his neck.

Within moments Jennifer was sitting on the kitchen floor, vigorously drying off a very ebullient and grateful puppy, who was trying its best to lick its benefactor, beside itself with a joy that went beyond the exhilaration of being clutched from the jaws of certain death.

Totally unconcerned with her own state of dishevelment, the young woman cooed away as she fell

53

totally in love for the second time in her life. Jeff just watched from the side, shaking his head in amusement. I don't have any idea where that dog came from, he thought, but I sure pity the person who would try to take it away from Jenny.

Later in the morning Jennifer found the house from where the puppy had roamed. Not only were they delighted to give the pup to Jenny, but offered her the rest of the same litter to go with him!

By the time Jeff came home for lunch, Jenny had named the puppy. "I'm calling him Moses because I saved him from the bullrushes," she asserted with great passion. "Jeff," she added thoughtfully, "I guess it's all right to use a biblical name, isn't it?"

Jeff thought of the Great Dane who shared a part in his youth. "Well, I grew up with a dog named Caleb. I guess if my dad thought it was okay to use that name, we can call our dog Moses," he responded as his wife hugged the dog and squealed happily.

For his part, Moses had in some mystical way, far beyond human understanding, become bonded in an immutable attachment to Jenny and seemed to assume that she was now the entire purpose of his life. Somehow this whole thing needs to be turned into one of those great sermon examples, Jeff thought as he watched Jenny prepare lunch with her one free hand.

As Jeff sat finishing his lunch, he looked over at this beautiful, bubbly creature the Lord had given him as wife. "Jenny, I had coffee this morning with your dad," he commented.

"He went to Billings today," she responded happily. "There is some big Masonic meeting that he and a bunch of the men went to. Mom said that he will be gone overnight, so they can't come for dinner tonight.

"He must have left pretty early for you to catch up with him at Tiny's," she added.

"Well, he talked to me about you getting involved in helping out with Job's Daughters. It seems that Charlie Miller's daughter is moving away and they need someone to guide the group. They all seem to think that you would be a great advisor, and your dad asked me if it would be acceptable for them to talk to you about it. What do you think?" he asked.

Jenny brightened up as he talked. "I just can't believe that Edna is leaving Badger Lake! I mean, she has been the Jobie leader for ever and ever," she exclaimed. "I would love to get involved again, Jeff. I was really into it before I went away to college. Do you really think it would be all right for me to do it?" she asked.

"Jenny, what I know about Job's Daughters could fit into a communion cup," he responded. "Fill me in on it a little, will you?"

"Gosh, Jeff," she replied. "It's been a long time since I even thought about it. First, its regular membership is for girls from ages 11 to 20. If a girl gets married, say at 17, she becomes what is called a Majority Member if she stays in it. Membership is restricted to girls who are relatives of Master Masons. We called our meeting room the BETHEL, which means Holy Place, and we wore grand robes that were supposedly worn by the women in the days of Job. I was an Honored Queen when I was a senior, and I guess I'm still a past Honored Queen.

"Let's see," she continued. "The whole thing is based on having an organization that teaches Masonic values to young girls—you know, like reverence for God and respect for parents and for the flag, the law, and our national leaders—and for becoming honorable wives," she said as she curtsied with a grand smile.

"Jen, what's the tie-in to the book of Job?" Jeff asked.

"Well," she answered, "the Job thing is based on the book of Job, and the motto came from Job 42:15: 'In all the land were no women found so fair as the daughters of Job, and their father gave them inheritance among their brethren.'

"A lot of the ritual and stuff is kind of dull," she commented with a little laugh, "but there's a lot of fun and a lot of sentimental things expressed in the rites showing how we are to overcome the trials and tribulations we encounter through life. It's all about striving for higher ideals and goals for our lives. A lot of it is quoted out of the Bible, and we sing hymns that say a lot of the same things."

"Honey, how much involvement does Job's Daughters have with the Masons themselves?" he inquired.

"There is always a Master Mason from the Bethel Guardian Council around," she replied. "There's a Control Council consisting of only adults. The head of the Council is a woman who has the title of Bethel Guardian. She is the one who always runs things as far as the girls are concerned. That's what Edna was and what they want me to be. It's just a fancy name for advisor.

"But as far as the local Masons, there is a lot of involvement," she acknowledged. "Each Bethel tries to relate to the Masonic groups it is tied to through the parents of the girls, and they in turn are expected to introduce the girls to the merits of future membership in the adult Masonic groups like The Eastern Star. We were encouraged to be examples of purity and charity and to influence our fathers, brothers, and friends . . . and future husbands," she emphasized, "to become interested with Freemasonry.

"But, Jeff," she explained, "the members themselves manage the actual business and affairs of the Bethel, and that helps give them confidence and abilities to prepare them for the future, too."

"Well, sounds like pretty wild stuff to me," Jeff charged with a grin. "But I guess it'll be duck soup to an old pro like you. Go for it if you want to, honey," he said to her delight.

Chapter
3

J eff left the house and walked across the church lawn, heading for the street. His eyes scanned the lines of the old church, resting finally on the cross atop the tall steeple. He reflected on the peace he felt as he worked around this place. Jeff's office was in a side extension of the sanctuary where the original Sunday school classes met. He had windows on two walls, giving him an easy view of both the Education Building and his house. Many of the books which the previous pastors had gathered over the years still filled the shelves across the inside wall. Jeff had spent many hours browsing through them, often lost for hours over a special find.

He smiled at the sight of the two-story Education Building as he turned the corner of the yard. He was pleased that although it was quite modern in style, it blended well with the original building. I'm so glad that it was already built and waiting, he thought. It makes it so much easier to reach the people comfortably. He couldn't imagine how he would ever handle the people without it, since the church was really bustling these days. Sunday morning attendance was always over 200 now, and the old church sanctuary was bursting at its seams each service. He had mentioned to the board that they might consider going to two morning services this fall if trends continued, and they were excited at the prospect of the obvious success the young minister was having in the community. People who came to check him out were returning with their whole families. Charlie Miller, the Church Treasurer, was elated with the increased revenues and was actually planning for some badly needed repairs that had been shelved for years.

Jeff crossed the street and glanced over at the huge red brick Masonic building. Its front entrance was centered on a three-sided set of concrete steps with nine levels. He had counted them one day, wondering if they held some mystical significance. Over the steps, two large white pillars held up a peaked white canopy or cover at the building roof height, with the letters A.F. & A.M. across its face.

He had attended a special meeting there earlier in the month when Jennifer was seated as the advisor or Bethel Guardian of the Job's Daughters and was surprised to see such an ornate interior with elaborate woodwork throughout. A reception for Jenny was held in the basement social hall, where the girls in the Job's Daughters waited on everyone in grand style, at least for Badger Lake.

He walked east toward the main business street on his way to his father-in-law's office. As he turned the corner onto Broadway, he almost knocked over Mick Sterling coming out of the Citizen's State Bank building. Grabbing the older man as he headed for the sidewalk, he apologized profusely.

"I'm so sorry, Mick," he cried. "I can't believe I just did that!"

Betty Sterling came out the door just behind them. "Goodness gracious, Mick! Are you all right, love?" she asked as she brushed his coat front with obvious concern. "Please, love," she cried with a bit of a smile, "pick on someone just a bit smaller than this huge bully next time, will you, dear?"

Jeff was beside himself with remorse, and it wasn't until both his friends were laughing with good humor at his terrible discomfort that he relaxed and broke into a grin.

"If there is ever another war," Mick joked, "call me right away, will you, and let me know what army you're in. I want to be sure I'm on your side!" He turned to his wife and took her arm, bent over in an exaggerated fashion. "Take me home, will you, love?" he asked his wife. "Or at least to the hospital emergency room."

Jeff loved this special couple and laughed with them as they took off down the street. Betty and Mick were transplants from England. After retiring from his career as a Flight Commander in the RAF, they came to America and spent a year or two traveling across the country. Somehow they eventually selected Badger Lake as the place where they wanted to spend their "golden years." Both were devout

Christians, Jeff realized during their first prayer time together, and had started attending his church regularly soon after he became pastor.

They walked briskly about town a great deal, and he often ran into them during his morning jogs and would then always walk a few hundred yards, fellowshipping with them. In the five years or so they had been living in Badger Lake, they had become well-liked regulars among the townspeople, with their good humor and friendly dispositions. Several mornings a week they would come to the church and spend several hours praying at the altar. Jeff watched them as they walked down the street, arm-in-arm, chatting away like two teenagers in love. He smiled and thought about how he and Jenny would look 45 years from now.

A few moments later he turned into the storefront offices of Roy Wallace. As usual, Roy was on the phone and waved him in from his seat with a welcome smile.

On the wall behind Roy's desk was an old and worn wooden plaque. In its upper left corner appeared a square and compass. In the center was an inscription. Though the letters were faded and darkened, the message was still clear. Jeff looked beyond Roy as he continued in his phone conversation and slowly read the words:

THE MEASURE OF A MASON

To wear the SQUARE and act upon it in all his daily deeds; to meet all men upon the LEVEL and judge them in accordance with the COMPASS OF TRUTH and CHARITY; to be loyal to his ORDER and ever MASTER of himself. To travel ever EAST-WARD from the feeble LIGHT of an ENTERED APPRENTICE toward the glorious LIGHT of WIS-DOM; and finally to be prepared for the final PASSWORD giving entrance to the presence of THE GRAND MASTER OF THE SUPREME ORDER OF THE UNIVERSE.

Roy looked up from his call while Jeff's eyes were still on the plaque. "That was my dad's for many years before he gave it to me when I opened this office," he said. "I've reread those words a thousand times since they were first on the wall in his study and now on this wall. They have a character, a powerful vitality that's all their own, don't they?" he commented. "I've molded my life around them. They really speak of what a true and loyal Mason is all about."

Jeff's first thought had been that although the message was one of encouraging a life dedicated to doing good, he would personally be more interested in molding his own life around that of Jesus Christ. However, that would be best left unsaid, he thought. "It's pretty impressive, Roy," he responded. "I'm sure your dad was proud to see it on your wall."

Roy nodded his agreement and smiled tightly. "My father was a hard man, both on his family and on himself, but when he died, Masons came from all over the state to attend his funeral. His business matters were in order and his affairs were all settled by his prearranged instructions within 30 days of his death. My mother didn't have to worry a single day of her life after he went to that Grand Lodge in the heavens. He had seen to it that everything would be provided for his family.

"Well," he continued with a deep sigh, "that's the mark of a Master Mason. A life built brick upon brick in an orderly structure."

Roy waved his hand across the tidy office where he had worked each day for so many years. The words flowed out from the normally taciturn man. "I guess that's why I'm so comfortable here. The insurance business is sort of like Freemasonry," he declared. "This business is built client by client, one family at a time, and one need at a time. Just look at the Masonic building down the street from you. It was built by a fraternity of builders, brick by brick, act upon act. It's a living testimony to both personal and Masonic achievement for everyone who was involved. That's why they used brick," he reflected. "I would expect that the Lord is going to look very seriously at those kinds of things, what each of us has contributed, day by day, to make this world a better place because of us having been in it."

The older man paused for a moment and then looked back up at his son-in-law with a broad smile. "When the Scriptures talk about us being co-workers with Christ, Jeff, this is what it means."

"Well, that's kind of what I wanted to talk to you about, Roy," the young man explained. "Jenny and I have been talking, and ever since she has been active in Job's Daughters again, she's wanted me to look into perhaps joining the Lodge so I can be more involved in her stuff. She suggested I talk to you," he concluded.

Roy, who had been leaning back comfortably in his chair, clambered out of it and came around the desk, grinning broadly from ear to ear. With eyes misted over with emotion, he took his son-in-law's hands in his own. "My, my! I can't begin to tell you what a thrill it is for me to hear those words from your lips. I don't know how many levels of joy a man is allowed in this life, but I have had my fill today. God is surely faithful," he exclaimed.

Over the next hour or so, Roy gave Jeff the basics of the Masonic story and grandly extolled the benefits which he could expect from Freemasonry. At great length he eagerly answered the many questions posed by the younger man.

As they finished, he took the young man by the hand again and spoke to him in a somber tone. "Remember, Jeff, it's a very rigid requirement that you personally seek membership, on your own, without pressure from anyone. I know that I'm not going to be able to sleep a single night until that glorious moment you are made a brother, and will be constantly pressuring you, so I'm going to ask you to talk to two other men in town who will guide you properly and orderly in your quest.

"You have two godly Masons on the church board," he continued. "They are Steve Hanson and Charlie Miller. Go see them both in the next day or two and ask them the same questions you've asked me. Let them instruct you from their own perspectives. If you still have a single question unanswered, I'd be greatly surprised. But if you do, come back and we'll get the answers.

"If you're completely satisfied, I'll help you formally petition the Lodge for membership," he concluded as he embraced Jeff warmly. "It's a day to celebrate! Let's call Jenny and Ruth and I'll spring for a good steak tonight down at the Rail's End, in Dillon. The Badger Lake Insurance Brokerage is closed for the rest of the day," he announced grandly.

◆

Steve Hanson had lost most of his hair before he turned 30. An extremely athletic man whose wiry frame and bursting energy belied the fact that he had just turned 50, Steve seemed happiest leading the several dozen church youngsters over hill and dale in some church youth outing. The Hansons' only child, a son, graduated with a 4.0 grade point average and was accepted two years ago in the pre-med program at Stanford, where he was working on his studies in preparing to become a doctor.

When Jeff entered the drugstore, Steve shouted a grand hello from the back, where the pharmacy was elevated enough from the rest of the store that he was able to have a clear view of the entire drugstore. Jeff reflected that in what was normally a one-man shop, the advantage was more than likely a planned necessity.

Jeff worked his way through the aisles to a counter just below the pharmacy, where the druggist was now waiting with his usual warm smile. "If you're looking for a prescription, Jeff, I'm sorry to tell you I don't have any with your name on it. You've come to the wrong place. You two are just too healthy. What can I do for you?" he asked with a good-natured grin.

"Actually, Steve, I need some advice," Jeff answered. "Roy and I have been speaking about Masonry. He suggested that I talk further about it with you. I know he and Jenny would both like me to join, but I'm just not sure. I know you're a Mason and I need someone to come out from behind the veil and tell me about it. It appears to be some kind of mystery that isn't a mystery to anyone except me," he laughed.

"Well, it really isn't a mystery at all, Jeff," Steve responded. "It's just that one of the cardinal rules in the craft is that we are forbidden to openly solicit or invite anyone to join the Lodge. Candidates have to come in of their own free will, without our persuasion. The idea is that someone should be drawn into the fellowship by our example, not by how good we are at recruiting.

"It doesn't mean that I can't talk to you about why I'm a Mason if you're really interested in knowing," he continued. "I'm really excited that you asked me. It's just like when someone asks you about the church, I guess. We love to talk about things that we love."

Steve leaned over the counter and reflected a moment before he spoke. "Masonry is a large part of my life, Jeff. Like your father-in-law, I entered Freemasonry in the Blue Lodge here in Badger Lake, and like him, I'm a past Worshipful Master. That means that at one time we both served as the head of the Lodge, or its Worshipful Master. I also went through both the York and Scottish Rites and I'm a Noble in the Shrine. Right now Charlie Miller is the Worshipful Master of the Badger Lake Lodge."

Steve walked around to Jeff's side of the counter. "I'm proud of my membership. It makes me a better man and a better husband and father. It also gives me a whole world full of brothers, real true brothers in every sense of the word. They might say that blood is thicker than water, but I can truly tell you, Jeff, that Masonry is thicker than them both! It would sure be great to call you a brother, as well as pastor and friend."

"Well, I think you already are my brother and friend, Steve," the younger man responded. "I just don't want to have anything stand in the way of or conflict with my responsibilities to the church and the Lord. I know my wife and her family have been active in it for a long time. It's only that I have never even known anyone who was a Mason until I came here."

Steve answered quickly. "Nothing as moral and harmonious with religious principles as Masonry could ever cause that kind of conflict, Jeff. In fact, Masonry has made me a better Christian, but it's not a religion nor is it ever intended to be any substitute for religion.

"The only creed, if you want to call it that, is the requirement that its members believe in a Supreme Being. Some wise Mason once said that the necessity to believe in one Supreme Being is an ancient craft requirement to insure that if a man recognized the fatherhood of God, he could readily accept the concept of the brotherhood of men."

He laughed a bit. "I really didn't make that up, Jeff. It was in a newspaper insert we had published in the Butte paper a couple of years ago. It also said that the goal of Masonry was to make good men better. You can't get into trouble with those kinds of standards!"

"Well, I guess not," Jeff answered. "But I have to tell you, Steve, that I'm still concerned about the secret side of the Lodge."

"Look, Jeff, Freemasonry is not a secret society. We don't hide our existence nor our membership. That Lodge building is directly across the street from the church and it has a great big sign hanging in front."

Steve raised both hands as in surrender. "I mean why would an organization which has its roots in brotherly love and helping others try to be secret?" he asked.

"Well, I didn't mean secret in that way, Steve," Jeff responded quietly. "I meant the oaths and things."

Steve looked up for a long moment at this man who stood there towering over him with such a quizzical, innocent look. Turning to go back around the counter, he beckoned to Jeff with a smile. "Come on back into the pharmacy and let's have a cup of coffee while I try to explain a few things. I have a feeling this might take a little while."

After they had each poured a cup of coffee, Steve offered Jeff one of two high stools at the upper counter in the pharmacy, where he could watch for customers. As they sat down, he leaned comfortably on the counter and turned his head to his visitor. "Jeff, let me try to explain why those oaths are there. First, Masonry actually started with the master builders of those great cathedrals and churches that were built throughout Europe during what we sometimes think of as the 'Dark Ages.' Those craftsmen were there helping the churches with their skills way back then, and we still do in many of the same ways today. So much of the work at our own church has been done by men operating under these principles.

"These builders were called Freemasons because they were a special class of worker, not subject to servitude or taxation, but freely traveled from country to country while most of the rest of the working class were in bondage, working almost as slaves.

"The Freemasons were highly protective of their craft and sought to keep their numbers small and their wages high. Obviously, they had to bring in and train new men, called apprentices, and teach them the skill required to maintain the high quality of their craft. When they had achieved the level of Master of their craft, they could then go out and direct the work of others. They were like the first construction superintendents.

"Now let me ask you a question, Jeff," Steve directed. "Assume that you were among these men in an age when there were no computers, phones, or cameras to create some lasting form of positive identification. How would you send these special classes or grades of artists across nation after nation and have them always be recognized as who they said they were?"

Jeff smiled. "Well, I instantly think of tattooing them with a special mark. But I guess that could be faked pretty easily once someone noticed that everyone at the same level of work on the same job had the same tattoo. It would have to be some kind of secret code that would indicate the level of skill at which each worker could legitimately operate," he answered rather smugly.

"Exactly! Now you can understand the origin of Masonry," Steve continued. "These men knew that if their craft was going to endure, those special passwords and things like coded handshakes, along with the other secrets of the craft, must be kept over generations . . . and the penalty for revealing any of them would have to be pretty severe." Steve sat back, pleased with having made it so clear to Jeff, who was leaning forward now in rapt attention.

"So the Freemasons formed Guilds or Lodges in which they preserved the craft and its secrets," he continued enthusiastically. "In those days there were three levels within the Lodge. The first group were the new trainees, or Entered Apprentices. Those who had passed their apprenticeship were called the Fellowcraft, or fellows of the craft. Finally, a man would be worthy enough to become a Master Mason, and on a rotation basis the Master Masons would be Masters of the Lodge.

"These men would hand out work assignments and be responsible not only for the men within the Lodge but their families as well, especially if something happened to the head of that family. They didn't have hospitalization plans or life insurance policies to fall back on—just honorable men who were true brothers. Today we Masons still take the charge to care for the widows, orphans, and families of our brothers in need as a very serious responsibility.

"Well, let's get back a few centuries," he grinned. "As time passed and the great age of cathedral building came to a close, so did the need for this elite fraternity of builders. But something unique had happened to those good men: They had become better men. So much better, in fact, that wherever they operated their Lodge, the local area was far the better for it. By that time many men who were merchants like Roy and myself were attracted to the Freemasons, having long admired their moral behavior, their business ethics and honesty, and their loyalty to their brethren.

"While history hasn't dotted every "i" in the matter, it appears that the old Freemasons, called Operative Masons, eventually accepted other moral, like-minded men into their fraternity who were not builders. These men were called Non-Operative or Speculative Masons, but were taught the same rituals and lessons of morality and man's brotherhood with man as were the operative members.

"In time the membership changed in its percentages, until today Freemasonry has become totally Speculative. Yet through all the generations since the Operative Lodges opened up to others, the old rituals were stringently maintained and are retained in their original form today."

Steve paused for a moment. "Do you want to know what brought me into Masonry, Jeff?" he asked.

As Jeff nodded vigorously, he continued, turning his full body to face the young pastor. "I saw Masonry as a place where the lowest-paid auto factory worker could put on a clean shirt and sit in the Lodge at the elbow of Henry Ford himself and be his equal. Did you know that the United States Declaration of Independence, the actual document itself, was written on a Masonic white Lambskin Apron, prepared by our Masonic brothers who helped prepare that precious cornerstone of our society? Some of the finest Christian men I knew, like my own uncle, were Masons. They never bragged on it, but just lived its principles with honor.

"I promised myself that if I joined a Lodge and found its members acting in any way that was in conflict with my principles and moral standards, I would leave it without a second thought. I am happy to say that there has never been a single circumstance at this Lodge or any other I have ever attended to cause me to reconsider my membership.

"Take this town and Lodge," he added quickly. "We have a number of civic groups here that I have belonged to at one time or another, but while they helped in the community and brought me in touch with others, they didn't encourage true brotherly love the way the Lodge does. When I became a Mason, I found that it required more time and work than any other organization. But I also learned that the more I put into the Lodge, the more I received in return. Nothing worthwhile comes without sacrifice. Any man who becomes a Masonic Brother and puts forth his best efforts will not be disappointed. Not only will he become an integral member of a great and diverse fraternity, but by learning the lessons of life taught so wonderfully in our ritual, he can become the type of person all good men admire," he asserted.

"I want my own son to become a Mason as soon as he is of age, and I want to encourage you, Jeff, if you have any interest in joining, to do it right away," Steve added. "It is the most enjoyable and enlightening part of my entire life. I know if you had asked Dick Taylor about it, he would have given you the same encouragement. It certainly was and will continue to be an enriching part of his life."

Steve reached over to a pile of magazines sitting on the counter. "Here," he remarked as he tossed one of the smaller ones in front of Jeff, "That's the *Scottish Rite Journal* for August. *The cover picture is of Roy Rogers, a 33rd Degree Mason*, the very highest in the Rite. You have to agree that he represents the epitome of honesty, decency, and faith in God and country. Roy Rogers is what we Masons call 'a Mason's Mason,' Jeff. That's the kind of man you would call brother if you were a Mason, too."

Their conversation was interrupted as several ladies arrived in the store. Steve jumped up as he cried, "Oh oh! I promised to fill a prescription for Mrs. Arntsen and here she is already. Entertain them for a minute or two, Jeff," he pleaded as he disappeared into the rows of medicine filled shelves.

The next morning, as Jeff jogged his way back toward town, he turned into the Grange yard, where he saw Charlie Miller's pickup. Charlie's day started early, and he was usually in and out of the cafe long before Jeff arrived each morning.

Tom Adams, an usher at church and one of the employees at the Grange, greeted him when he entered through the shipping door in the rear of the shop. "Hi, Jeff! Give up preaching? In to pick up some grain for the stock?" he asked with a good-natured grin.

"No," Jeff laughed. "Just in to see Charlie. Is he around?" he asked.

"Back in his office," Tom answered as he pointed toward the glassed-in office, where Jeff could see the back of Charlie's head as the man leaned over his desk. "See you later, Jeff. I've got a long day and a lot of feed to deliver," Tom proclaimed as he walked through the loading doors.

Jeff walked back to the office and tapped on the glass window of the door as he walked in. "I thought I'd take a little breather before I try jogging the rest of the way to town," he declared as Charlie Miller glanced up with a pleased look of surprise. "Do you have a few minutes, Charlie?"

"Great to see you, Jeff," he responded as he rose to shake hands with his visitor. "Steve told me you might be by. Lord knows I've watched you jog by the place often enough. My wife has been on me to lose some of this well-deserved gut by following your example. You sure are a tough example for us old guys to follow. Next preacher around here is going to have to be old and overweight to get my vote," he laughed with great delight.

Charlie Miller had been the Manager of the Badger Lake Cooperative Grange since the Grange opened its doors in 1957. He had hired on at the Grange right out of school at Missoula, where they recruited him in 1952. He worked in their management program and was Assistant Manager at the Dillon Grange when he was offered the job in Badger Lake at the time the position first opened up. The son of a rancher, he knew the needs of the stockmen whom he serviced and they trusted him implicitly.

Charlie Miller had married his childhood sweetheart, had lived his whole life in Southwest Montana, and had considered himself to be the happiest, most successful man he could ever imagine. He was the Worshipful Master of the Badger Lake Masonic Lodge, and with his friends he had risen through both the York and Scottish Rites. He was also a Shriner. He had had only one single employer his entire career and would soon have 40 years of service behind him.

Charlie motioned for Jeff to take a seat with him at the large leather sofa across from his desk. "Sit down and let's talk, Jeff," he said as he lowered himself into the well-worn couch. "I have been meaning to stop in to let you know just how pleased I am with your ministry here. My whole family is excited about church again," he grinned broadly.

Jeff fought a losing battle trying hard not to grin back at this man whose contagious smile forced a response in kind. "I truly appreciate your encouragement, Charlie. It's so great to be at Badger Lake! The work is really growing this summer."

Charlie leaned toward his visitor. "Jeff," he spoke quietly in a solemn tone, "Let's get right to the point. I know why you stopped in to see me. We hardly need phones in Badger Lake for news to get around. That's doubly true when it involves the church or the Lodge. I know that you've been asking about Freemasonry. I don't know when I've ever been more excited and overanxious about someone inquiring about the Lodge. I can't think of *any* young man I know who has been a better candidate. You already exemplify the model of a fully developed Mason. You are the kind of person that can really bring the Masonic experience into full blossom. What can I do to help you step into fellowship with us?" he asked.

"I guess I'm just nervous about what's behind the veil," the young man remarked. "I suppose I'm making a lot out of a little. Jenny is so happy with her Job's Daughter thing. I want to be more of a part of that side of her life. Just tell me what you think would help me make up my mind in the matter, okay? You talk and I'll listen," he said with a little smile of his own.

The older man smiled back. "Well, first let me tell you why I am a Mason, Jeff. My dad became a Mason almost 50 years ago over in Bozeman. I have always greatly respected and admired his devotion to the Lodge. He was a successful stockman and rancher who was extremely active in the fellowship and was raised to the honorary level of the 33rd

Degree. Even today, in his 90's his mind is as sharp as ever and he has an understanding of the deeper things in the Craft that I may never figure out.

"My grandfather was also a Mason, raised in 1898 in Great Falls, and his father, my great-grandfather became a Mason almost 20 years earlier, in South Pass City, Wyoming, in 1879. That was the first Masonic Lodge in the whole Wyoming territory.

"Even my wife's father and grandfather were active in Masonry, so you can see that my whole family has been quite involved. I'm proud to say that my son and my son-in-law are both active Masons.

"In fact, Jeff," he continued, "the very organization I work for, the Grange, is a Masonic agricultural cooperative originally put together by Masons who felt the strong need for farmers and ranchers to join together to the benefit of their specialized needs. It eliminated the middlemen who were price-gouging and taking the profits away from those who earned them. These customers aren't just customers—they each own a share of the cooperative and are really my bosses. A good many of them are my Masonic brothers.

"Thinking about it now, I can't think of a single action or thought I saw or learned in Masonry that has been in conflict with my faith, my family, or my country. In fact, most Masons I know are men who are the cornerstones of their communities and churches. They are family men who live by the ideals of the Golden Rule. They are the best kinds of men—men like your father-in-law, who are the backbone of our fraternity."

Jeff was riveted to his every word. Charlie had one trait that reminded him of his own father: He looked Jeff squarely in the eye as he spoke, intent on firmly drilling the words of his testimony home to the very heart.

Charlie persisted. "Freemasonry is what made this nation great and it is what built the very church in which you minister. It built the young lady with whom you now share your life and it is the stuff great men are known by—men like George Washington and Sam Houston and Ben Franklin.

"Right here in Montana, the men who settled here, risking all they had to open up the mines and the mountains, many of those pioneers were Masons. In fact, the first white men known to step foot into Montana were the members of the Lewis and Clark expedition in 1805 and 1806. Both Lewis and Clark were brother Masons."

Charlie chuckled as he continued. "Most people don't know this, but Lewis had his closest brush with death right here in Montana at the hands of a Masonic brother who mistook Lewis for an elk and put a heavy rifle ball through his thigh. Lewis almost died from it. Had the guy been a better shot, he would have changed the course of history and had a side of meat a whole lot tougher than elk," he roared as he leaned back with laughter.

Jeff roared along in response, thinking that he was determined that he would look up the details of that expedition someday before he died and try to find out if that story was really true.

With tears still in his eyes, Charlie fell back into his discourse on the merits of the Craft. "Just last year, former President Gerald Ford, a 33rd Degree Mason, spoke at our State Reunion. Even President Reagan, before he left office, was made a Mason 'on sight,' which is quite an honor for any man, including a President! Back a few years ago I went to the National Convention for our own church denomination when it was in Dallas and the President of the Convention was a Mason. Even the President of the University where you met Jenny is a Mason. These are the kinds of men with whom you would share brotherhood."

The older man leaned forward with great intent, his brow ridged with deep furrows of concentration as he spoke. "The Great Book says, 'By their fruits ye shall know them,' and you can always use that guide to judge a Mason—by his acts and by the many benefits that flow from them. Then you will know what type of men are Masons and you will be proud to be counted among their number."

Charlie stood and took a small booklet and a sheet of paper from his desk. He turned and faced the young minister who had just risen from his seat.

"Jeff," he began, "as a board member of the Badger Lake First Baptist Church and as a longtime close friend and associate of your wife's family and as the Worshipful Master of the Badger Lake Masonic Lodge, I encourage you to take this little book on gaining membership in the Lodge, along with this enclosed form, called a Petition. Take them home to read.

"When you are impressed to join with us as a true brother," he instructed, "fill out the Petition and give it to your father-in-law. After he brings it to the

Lodge as your sponsor, we will send a Petition committee of two men to interview you. After they report back with what I expect will be a good report, we will arrange to bring you into membership at a special meeting."

Chapter
4

J ennifer reached up and gave Jeff one of her I-love-you-forever kisses. "Sweetheart, my mom is coming over and we're going to go over to the Lodge in a bit and get the refreshments ready downstairs for the end of your initiation. She'll keep me company tonight, so I guess the next time I'll see you again you'll be a real live Mason."

Jeff drew her close to him for a giant hug. Tripping over the ever-enthusiastic Moses, he headed out the door into the crisp fall night. Over the last several months he had continued to study the merits of membership in the Lodge, and had finally concluded that if he were to spend the majority of his ministry among these people, he was going to have to do a little more conforming. While he hadn't seen much to discourage joining, his wife's family was certainly encouraging him to "become a better man." In fact, he had privately felt that his in-laws had gone a bit beyond simple encouragement. But then, he could understand their motives in it. Not having a son of his own must be hard on a man like Roy, he thought. Maybe this would help to make up for it a bit.

He walked to the Lodge with slow, measured steps, but with his long stride it still took just a few short minutes. He could see that there was a good cluster of cars parked in the area for the special meeting. Steve Hanson had told him that he was the only initiate at tonight's meeting—in fact the first for a number of months—and had warned the young man that the entire Lodge membership would probably be there for the event.

As Jeff climbed the grand set of steps to the entrance of the building, Roy Wallace was already coming through the equally imposing set of entry doors. "Well, my son, I welcome you to the portals of the eternal light of Masonry," he said with deep emotion as he held the door for his son-in-law to enter. Jeff was sure that Roy had practiced that statement before he spoke it on the steps outside.

Roy was dressed to the teeth and bursting with intense pride. Earlier in the day he had stopped at their house to tell Jeff that he would be sitting in for the Worshipful Master during Jeff's initiation, so that he would have the privilege of officiating at his entry into the Craft. Charlie Miller had insisted he do so, and Roy had closed down his office for several days in order to work on the memorization that was apparently necessary for the event.

The two men were immediately immersed in the crowd of Masons milling about the entry hall. Jeff pushed his way through the throng behind Roy, shaking hands and greeting the many men he knew from church and town. With his height, he stood a head above most in the crowd, and as soon as he was noticed, everyone pressed in, each one wanting to welcome him personally. He guessed that there were close to a hundred men there in the hallway. They finally worked their way to an anteroom, just to the side of two great doors that opened into the actual Lodge room where the ritual would take place. Both Steve and Charlie were with a number of men waiting there, and they all greeted him with great enthusiasm.

"Jeff!" Charlie shouted over the din. "In just a few moments we're going to begin assembling the Lodge inside those doors. Once we have officially opened the Lodge and finished the regular business, your initiation will become the main point of the rest of the time, and we will begin the process of introducing you to the instruction and ritual required of membership."

"So just relax," Steve interrupted, "and leave the driving to us," he laughed. "We haven't lost an initiate yet. Remember, everyone is here to see you become entered as a brother Mason!"

Roy introduced him to several men who were representing the State Grand Lodge, where Roy was an officer. They were there, he was sure, out of respect for his father-in-law, who had been raised to the 33rd degree during the summer.

At a call from one of the men whom Jeff presumed to be a Lodge officer, the men began filtering into the Lodge room. Soon Jeff was the lone occupant of the anteroom. One of his elderly parishioners, Raymond Claudy, stepped back through the inner door on several occasions and appeared to be checking on him. He informed Jeff in a whisper that he was the Lodge Tiler and was responsible to keep guard at the door. From his almost-fierce demeanor, it was a job he apparently took quite seriously, Jeff mused.

After what seemed like an eternity of waiting, the elder man opened the inner door and four men filed out into the anteroom. The inner door was closed again by brother Claudy.

Jeff knew one of the men, Lee Richards, who was the manager of the Citizen's State Bank, where he had almost knocked down Mick Sterling last summer. Lee smiled nervously as he stepped forward of the three others. "Jeff, I'm going to be making a candidate's statement and administering what we call the interrogatory to you right now. I'm the Lodge Secretary and I am accompanied by Stan Fields here, who is the Junior Deacon, Tom Adams, who is the Senior Steward, and Duane here, who is the Junior Steward. Just answer normally as I ask you several questions later, okay?" he asked. Jeff nodded his consent as the Lodge officers stepped further into the anteroom with him.

Lee cleared his throat and began his prepared statement. "Reverend Moore, somewhat of your motives in applying for admission into our ancient and honorable fraternity we have learned from the declaration, over your signature, contained in your petition; but in order that you may not be misled as to the character or the purpose of the ceremonies in which you are about to engage, the Lodge addresses to you these preliminary words of advice.

"Freemasonry," he declared, "is far removed from all that is trivial, selfish, and ungodly. Its structure is built upon the everlasting foundation of that God-given law, the Brotherhood of Man, in the family whose father is God. Our ancient and honorable Fraternity welcomes to its doors and admits to its privileges worthy men of all creeds and of every race, but insists that all men shall stand upon an exact equality, and receive its instructions in a spirit of due humility, emphasizing in demeanor, in conduct, in ceremony, and in language the helpless, groping nature of man at his birth and his need of reliance upon divine guidance through all the transactions of life."

Lee paused for a moment and caught his breath. Jeff was amazed that the man was reciting this whole thing by memory. With a renewed sparkle in his eye, Lee went on: "You will here be taught to divest your mind and conscience of all the vices and superfluities of life, and this Lodge into which you are now to be admitted expects you to divest yourself of all those worldly distinctions and equipments which are not in keeping with the humble, reverent, and childlike attitude which it is now your duty to assume, as all have done before you."

Lee hesitated again for a brief moment, then continued. "Every candidate, previous to his reception, is required to give his free and full assent to the following interrogatories, in a room adjacent to the Lodge."

Lee looked directly at Jeff and inquired, "Do you seriously declare, upon your honor, that unbiased by the improper solicitation of friend and uninfluenced by mercenary motives, you freely and voluntarily offer yourself as a candidate for the mysteries of Freemasonry?"

"Yes, I do," Jeff answered quietly.

"Do you seriously declare," Lee asked, "upon your honor, that you are prompted to solicit the privileges of Freemasonry by a favorable opinion conceived of the institution, a desire for knowledge, and a sincere wish of being serviceable to your fellow creatures?"

"Yes, I do," Jeff repeated.

"Do you seriously declare, upon your honor, that you will cheerfully conform to all the ancient usages and established customs of the Fraternity?" he asked.

"Yes, I do," Jeff responded again.

"Finally, do you believe in the existence of one ever-living and true God and in a transition to a future life?"

Again Jeff replied, "Yes, I do."

With the look of a man who had just completed a job well done, Lee smiled broadly at Jeff and nodded his approval at his answers to the questions. He then turned sharply and returned quickly to the Lodge through the doors held open by the elderly brother.

Stan Fields stepped forward with a grim look. He was a short, thin man with a naturally pinched-up face that made him look sinister even when he was smiling. "Reverend Moore, as you have given satisfactory answers to the questions propounded, it becomes my pleasing duty . . ." The words droned past Jeff's active mind as the man went through another recitation on the purity and beauty of the ceremonies. He was watching the two Stewards as their eyes roamed the details of the wall behind him. As their eyes swung back suddenly to the Junior Deacon, Jeff tuned back in with them, and just in time, he thought.

"To impress this truth more forcefully on your mind," Stan was saying, "it is now necessary that you divest yourself of a portion of your clothing and be clothed in a garment furnished by the Master of this Lodge, similar in form, character, and meaning to that which has been worn by all who have gone this way before. If you submit to this and are ready and willing to proceed, I will leave you in the hands of these true and trusted friends, who will see that you are properly prepared and duly presented."

Stan Fields stepped back a bit and tried an uncomfortable smile. "Jeff, I am going to ask you to suffer through this next little bit of discomfort with a stiff upper lip. Just remember that every single man in that Lodge room has gone through the exact same procedure. Please try to endure it with patience and a little humor."

Before Jeff was able to give a reply, the Junior Deacon spun on his heels and disappeared into the Lodge room. Now it was Tom Adams' turn. Along with his good friend, Win Johnson, Tom had taken

Jeff to the lake a number of times during the summer. Tom was probably the most competitive fisherman Jeff had ever met. He would become almost wild-eyed if Jeff or Win hooked a fish first or if someone else's catch was the biggest, and would stay out there for hours until he had achieved some advantage in quantity or quality. The last time out, Jeff had quietly slipped a near-trophy Brown back into the lake before Tom saw it and kept them there the rest of the day trying to outdo it. In all of it, Jeff enjoyed his times with Tom immensely.

Tom stepped forward, trying to suppress a satisfied smirk that was turning up the corners of his mouth. "Reverend Moore, you will now take off your suit coat, shoes, and socks, and remove your tie. Just place them on the chair there," he said, pointing to a seat nearby.

As Jeff quickly complied, he continued. "Now please remove your trousers, and here is a pair of proper drawers for you," he said with a flair as he passed on a pair of baggy pants handed to him by the other Steward, Duane.

"You will now unbutton the front of your shirt and slip your left arm out of your shirtsleeve and put it through the front of your shirt, so that your arm and breast are bare," he instructed as he stepped in to help Jeff figure out how to do what he had just been ordered to do.

As Jeff stepped into the baggy pants, he saw that one leg was cut short and rolled back at the left knee. Tom spoke softly to his friend. "Jeff, I am now going to blindfold you with a thing we call the hoodwink. Then I am going to put a loose rope around your neck that is called a cabletow. It will drag on the floor behind you. First, let me slide this slipper on your right foot," he said as he knelt down before him.

Moments later, as Tom finished his duties, Stan Fields returned. "Reverend Moore," he charged, "I am afraid that you are going to have to remove your wedding ring before proceeding into the Lodge."

Jeff almost ripped the hoodwink from his head in his panic. "What do you mean, remove my ring?" he gasped. "That ring represents my marriage vows, my fidelity to my wife. Why would you want me to take that off before continuing?"

"It has nothing to do with your wedding vows, I assure you, Jeff," he answered quickly. "It's just that you can't wear any metal during the ritual. Tom will keep it safe for you to put back on the moment you finish your vows inside."

Jeff, reluctant to get into some major battle over his intense disdain for the request, allowed them to assist him in removing the ring. The men led him to the door, where one of them rapped three times. Jeff assumed it was Stan Fields, but with the blindfold he had to guess at the activities around him. Soon someone responded with three distinct knocks from the other side and opened the door. "Who comes here?" asked a voice.

"The Reverend Jeffrey Moore," answered a voice he knew was Fields, "who has long been in darkness and now seeks to be brought to light and receive a part of the rights and benefits of this Worshipful Lodge, erected to God and dedicated to the Holy Saints John, as all brothers and fellows have done before."

The voice from inside asked, "Reverend Moore, is it of your own free will and accord?"

"It is," replied Jeff to the darkness.

"Brother Junior Deacon, is he worthy and well-qualified?" asked the voice.

"He is," responded Stan, who was at his arm.

"Duly and truly prepared?"

"He is."

"Of lawful age and properly vouched for?"

"He is."

"By what further right or benefit does he expect to gain admission?"

"By being a man, free born, of good repute and well-recommended," was the reply.

"Is he such?"

"He is."

"Since he is in possession of all these necessary qualifications, you will wait with patience until the Worshipful Master is informed of his request and his answer returned," said the voice as the door closed in front of them.

A few minutes passed until the door reopened and the voice spoke again. "Let him enter this Worshipful Lodge, in the name of God, and be received in due and ancient form."

Led by Stan Fields, and flanked by the two others, Jeff entered the Lodge, advancing until stopped by the man attached to the voice, who pressed a sharp pointed instrument against his bared breast.

"Reverend Moore, on entering this Lodge for the first time, I receive you on the sharp point of the compass pressing your naked left breast, which is to teach you, as it is a torture to your flesh, so should the recollection of it ever be to your mind and conscience, should you attempt to reveal the secrets of Masonry unlawfully." Upon that charge, the instrument was removed from his chest and the voice walked away from him, as did the two men directly behind him. A few moments went by until the voice returned and took him forward by the right arm until they stopped at the sound of what Jeff thought was a gavel sounding.

A voice he immediately identified as Roy Wallace's spoke with a resonance that Jeff thought must come from the acoustics of the Lodge room. "Let no one enter on so important a duty without first invoking the blessing of the Deity. Brother Senior Deacon, you will conduct the candidate to the center of the Lodge and cause him to kneel for the benefit of prayer."

Jeff was again led a number of steps forward and to the left slightly. There he was asked to kneel by the voice, whom he now knew was the Senior Deacon. Again there was a stir as someone else approached him and knelt by his side and began to pray. The moment he spoke, Jeff knew it was again his father-in-law.

"Vouchsafe Thine aid, Almighty Father of the Universe, to our present convention; and grant that this candidate for Masonry may dedicate and devote his life to Thy service, and become a true and faithful brother among us! Endue him with a competency of Thy divine wisdom, that by the secrets of our art he may be better enabled to display the beauties of brotherly love, relief, and truth to the honor of Thy Holy Name. Amen."

Jeff actually jumped when the entire Lodge room reverberated as all those in attendance responded, "So Mote It Be!" He had been so absorbed in the ritual that he had forgotten there were close to a hundred men watching him wander around blindfolded.

Roy stood, and taking Jeff by the right hand, he reached out and placed his left hand on Jeff's head. "Reverend Moore, in whom do you put your trust?" he asked.

Jeff immediately responded, "*In my Lord, Jesus Christ.*" Jeff heard a murmur of approval run through those in attendance.

After what Jeff thought was a significant pause, his father-in-law answered him, "Since your trust is in God, your faith is well-founded. Arise," he commanded as he assisted Jeff to his feet, "Follow your conductor and fear no danger."

With that pronouncement, Roy stepped back and the Senior Deacon reappeared at his side and proceeded to walk Jeff around the inner perimeter of the room, all the while reciting another portion of the ritual.

"Behold, how good and how pleasant it is for brethren to dwell together in unity! It is like the precious ointment upon the head, that ran down upon the beard, even Aaron's beard; that went down to the skirts of his garments, as the dew of Hermon, and as the dew that descended upon the mountains of Zion; for there the Lord commanded the blessing, even life forevermore."

At several junctures in the walk a gavel would sound close by, and when they finally came to a stop, another gavel sounded and a new voice asked, "Who comes here?"

The Senior Deacon began answering with the same responses that were given at the door prior to his entrance: "The Reverend Jeffrey Moore, who has long been in darkness and now seeks to be brought to light..."

Having finished the presentation at that spot, he was guided to yet another station, where the process was exactly repeated for the third time. From that point things became confusing for Jeff. He was taken to stand before what he thought was a seated Roy Wallace, where it was determined that he was still seeking light. From there he was passed back to the last station, where he was instructed in placing the heel of his left foot into the hollow of his right. It's going to be a long, long night, Jeff mused as he complied.

Led back to the center of the room, Jeff stood awaiting the next instruction. "The candidate is in order and awaits your further will and pleasure," announced his instructor.

Jeff listened as the sounds indicated that Roy Wallace had stepped down from his chair and was approaching him. "Reverend Moore," his father-in-law proclaimed, "before you can be permitted to advance any farther in Masonry, it becomes my duty to inform you that you must take upon yourself a solemn oath or obligation, appertaining to this degree, which I, acting as Master of this Lodge, assure you will not materially interfere with the duty that you owe to your God, yourself, family, country, or neighbor. Are you willing to take such an oath?"

"I am willing," responded the young minister.

"Brother Senior Warden," he resumed, "you will place the candidate at the altar in due form, which is by kneeling on his naked left knee, his right forming the angle of a square, his left hand supporting the Holy Bible, Square, and Compasses, his right hand resting thereon."

With the help of the other, Jeff worked his way into the position commanded by the Worshipful Master. Once in place, the instruction continued.

"Reverend Moore, you are now in position for taking upon yourself the solemn oath of an Entered Apprentice Mason, and if you are still willing to take the obligation, say I, pronounce your name in full, and repeat after me."

Roy paused for a moment, and at the sound of a gavel, the room came alive as all those present gathered around the altar.

Jeff began, "I, Jeffrey Moore . . ." and continued as he followed his prompts, "of my own free will and accord, in the presence of Almighty God and this worshipful Lodge, erected to Him, and dedicated to the Holy Saint John, do hereby and hereon most solemnly and sincerely promise and swear that I will always hale, ever conceal and never reveal, any of the arts, parts, or points of the hidden mysteries of Ancient Freemasonry which I have received, am about to receive, or may be hereafter instructed in, to any person unless it shall be to a worthy Brother Entered Apprentice, or within the body of a just and duly constituted Lodge of Masons;

and not unto him or them until, by strict trial, due examination, or lawful information, I shall have found him or them as lawfully entitled to the same as I am myself.

"Furthermore," he continued, "I do promise and swear that I will not write, indict, print, paint, stamp, stain, hew, cut, carve, mark, or engrave the same upon anything movable or immovable, whereby or whereon the least word, syllable, letter, or character may become legible or intelligible to myself or another whereby the secrets of Freemasonry may become unlawfully obtained through my unworthiness."

There was a silent pause for a moment until his father-in-law resumed the prompting. "All of this I most solemnly, sincerely promise and swear, with a firm and steadfast resolution to perform the same, without any mental reservation or secret evasion of mind whatever, binding myself under no less penalty than that of having my throat cut across, my tongue ripped out by its roots, and my body buried in the rough sand of the sea at low-water mark, where the tide ebbs and flows twice in twenty-four hours, should I ever knowingly violate this my Entered Apprentice obligation. So help me God, and keep me steadfast in the due performance of the same."

They certainly didn't leave anything out, Jeff speculated in the silent moment following the obligation.

Roy addressed him again. "In token of your sincerity, you will now kiss the Holy Bible on which your hand rests."

As Jeff finished obeying his instruction, he questioned him further. "In your present condition, what do you most desire?"

Jeff wanted to say he wished the whole thing would soon end, but gave the prompted response, "*Light*," instead.

Roy Wallace spoke to the full assembly. "Brethren, you will stretch forth your hands and assist me in bringing our newly made brother to true light in Masonry."

"In the beginning," he intoned, "God created the heavens and the earth. And the earth was without form and void, and darkness was upon the face of the deep. And God said, Let there be light, and there was *light*."

At the sound of the latter word *light*, all those present clapped once in unison and the hoodwink was snatched from Jeff's eyes. Now he could finally see where he was kneeling at the altar, with a beam of light shining directly down on it from above. In front of him stood Roy Wallace, dressed in what Jeff assumed were the trappings of his high office. Roy turned to one of the other men standing around the altar. "Brother Senior Deacon, I will now thank you to remove the cabletow, as we now hold this brother by a stronger tie."

As the rope was taken from around his neck, Roy turned back to him and continued on. While Jeff had hoped the ritual was basically over, he soon realized that there was a whole lot more, that he had just reached the entry level. Now, having passed through the obligation, he was next to learn a secret handshake called a grip which he was to use in being recognized as an Entered Apprentice. The Grip had the name of BOAZ and even that had to be spoken in a secret manner in order to detect any impostors.

Jeff concluded that while he appreciated the sincerity of everyone involved, he would highly doubt that someone would go so far out of his way as to secretly work his way into such a lengthy procedure as that which he was experiencing tonight.

Next Jeff was given a white Lambskin Apron whose pure and spotless surface, he was lectured, would be "an ever-present reminder of purity of life and rectitude of conduct, and when at last, after a life of faithful service, your weary feet shall have come to the end of life's toilsome journey and from your nerveless grasp shall have dropped forever the working tools of life, may the record of your life be as pure and spotless as this fair emblem which I place in your hands tonight, and when your trembling soul shall stand, naked and alone, before the Great White Throne, there to receive judgment for the deeds done while here in the body, may it be your portion to hear from Him who sitteth as the Judge Supreme the welcome words: Well done, thou good and faithful servant. Thou hast been faithful over a few things, I will make thee ruler over many things! Enter into the joy of thy Lord."

It was over an hour later that the meeting came to an end. Jeff's mind was still reeling from the minute details of the rest of the ritual that followed his initiation into membership. He felt that he would never sort out the gauge, gavel, tokens, secret handshakes, Greater and Lesser lights, and repetitions of almost everything.

Well, I must have done a decent enough job, since everyone seemed well pleased enough, he thought to himself. In fact, from the hearty congratulations from everyone immediately following the meeting, as the crowd was making a beeline for the refreshments downstairs, he judged that he must have given an outstanding performance. Either that or they were so thrilled to see the new pastor come into the fold that they were overjoyed. Of course, it may be that *they* are even more relieved than I am to get out of there tonight, he reasoned with a private grin.

Jeff slowly worked his way through the crowd of Lodge members and made his way to the serving table, where Jennifer, her mother, and several other ladies were chatting happily with Roy and his out-of-town friends who were standing there with him. They had yet to drive back up to Butte tonight, but wanted to take the time to have some pie and coffee with him before they left.

"Jeff, it was a great privilege to be here tonight for your entrance into the light of the Craft," Carl Montgomery said as they were seating themselves. "I can't remember an initiation that I've attended that was witnessed to by such a group of enthusiastic brethren. You are certainly highly thought of here, young man. It was especially significant for me to be able to witness Roy's son-in-law being entered into the Lodge." Carl smiled broadly at first Jeff and then the rest of the men gathered around the table. Out of the corner of his eye, Jeff could see Jenny watching from the serving table, beaming with pride.

Roy Wallace nodded along his approval as he reached over and laid his hand on Carl's arm. "I know that you have a lot to digest about Freemasonry, Jeff, but Carl is the Most Worshipful Grand Master of the State Lodge, as well as CEO of a major mining corporation. We are so grateful to have him here tonight."

"Well, thanks, Roy. I am the one who should be grateful," Carl returned. "I love to see the brotherhood and fellowship of these longtime Lodges. You know," he continued, "Badger Lake is one of the oldest Lodges in the territory. The cornerstone on this building says 5915, or 1915. But the Lodge was given its charter in 1895. Fellow Masons have been regularly meeting in this town for almost a hundred years. Pretty impressive."

By now most of the men present had gathered around the table, realizing that they were being treated to a bit of an impromptu message from their state leader.

Carl rose to the occasion. "Tonight, as I watched this young man go through that same rite through which each of us has passed, I had to reflect on what it was that brought him to petition for membership. You know, it made me look back on why I wanted to become a Mason."

"The fact is, I grew up surrounded by Masons. Nearly every adult male I knew was a member of the Craft, and they were all go-getters. Each was the kind of man I wanted to be. They were good husbands, good fathers, and solid citizens. Wherever there was a need these were the kind of men who met it. They served their country in times of war, and they served their communities and churches with a zeal sadly lacking elsewhere in the world, especially today."

He gazed around the room, making eye contact with every man within his sight. "These men whom I admired and loved most were proud to be Masons. They accepted one another and were always ready to lend a helping hand. They had a special dignity about them that I still seek to develop in my own life. It's the kind of bonding that has made this Lodge so strong for so many years."

He looked back to Jeff once again. "Jeff, I have been in business for over 50 years now, and have found that if a person is to be a success in life, he must have good self-esteem. Masonry builds this character trait, and one of the great advantages of being a Mason is the companionship with men like these men"—he motioned with his hand to indicate the men filling the room about them—"who stand at your side, ready and willing to help you whenever you or your family needs assistance. No matter where you go in the world, there will be that bond. Men whom you will have only met will stand as strong for you as your own father-in-law would." Carl rose from the table as he spoke the last words, indicating that the discourse was over. As he rose, the several others who had come with him stood also, shaking the hands of those around them.

"We have to run now," he said. "I've got an early flight out in the morning and it's a long drive home." After shaking hands with Jeff and a few others, he whispered a farewell to Roy and made his way over to the serving table, where he paid his respects to Jenny, Ruth, and the other ladies. Within moments he and his group had left, and as if on cue the rest of the Lodge began following their example.

Late into the night and long after Jenny had fallen off to sleep, Jeff stared at the ceiling of their bedroom. Moses had by now worked his way into the bedroom at night and was firmly established at the foot of the bed, on Jenny's side. As Jeff listened to the regular breathing of his little family, he reflected on the events of the night. It was certainly something else, he thought, and the words of the ritual were truly grand and noble, but Jeff knew down deep that something was missing there tonight. It finally dawned on him and he blushed in the dark from embarrassment as he realized that no one throughout the entire night had mentioned Jesus or what had happened to their lives when they found Jesus. It was the Lodge that was their transformer, not Christ!

Chapter
5

Jeff made the turn onto the four-lane at an easy pace. The weather was brisk and the cold air helped shake out the cobwebs of a long, sleepless night. He felt his tight muscles loosen up and he inhaled deeply as he picked up the pace. Jogging was not a companion sport, at least in his home. He had tried to interest Jenny in joining him in this daily regimen, but it wasn't her idea of either exercise or companionship. Nor was her three-times-a-week aerobics session in front of the television with her friends and Jane Fonda his idea of a workout, although he had to admit that Jennifer was in great shape.

The few times she came along with him were pleasant enough, but she certainly went at a different pace and could not work up the enthusiasm for any kind of exercise this early in the morning.

As he came back into the main section of town, he noticed Mick Sterling walking south along the street. Strange, he thought. That's the first time I've seen him out without Betty. I wonder if she's okay.

"Mick," he called out as he came up behind him. "Is everything okay? I've never seen you walking without Betty before."

"Oh, she's just fine," Mick smiled as the young man came alongside and slowed down to walk with him. "I'm only taking a little Saturday morning stroll and I just wanted to get a bit of time alone with you this morning. I need to talk to you privately about something, Jeff."

"Well, you don't have anyone in line ahead of you this time of the day," Jeff laughed. "What's wrong, Mick?" he asked as he realized that his friend was not responding in his usual good humor. The older man stopped walking and turned to face the young pastor.

Mick looked at Jeff in silence for a long moment, as though he were struggling to find the words. "Jeff, is it true, lad, that you've joined up with the Masons?"

Jeff was bewildered by the question and the grave look of this kindly man. "Yes, I did, Mick," he answered. "In fact, I became a member just last night. Why do you ask?"

"Well, I just couldn't believe it, that's all! Now that I've heard it from your own lips, I guess I have to believe it." Mick was apparently deeply upset. For the first time in their friendship, Jeff saw a steely look in Mick's eyes that reminded him that this thoughtful, gentle man had been a Wing Commander during wartime.

"I am just absolutely dumbfounded!" he continued with deep exasperation. "I pray to God, Jeff, that you don't die and have to face the wrath of a righteous and holy God in your present state of idolatry and sin!"

Mick Sterling was at least a full foot shorter than Jeff Moore, but it seemed to Jeff that Mick had delivered that last statement nose-to-nose, and he jumped back as though struck by electricity. "What on earth are you talking about, Mick?" he cried out in despair. "I just joined a social group that half the town belongs to and that's *all* I did!"

Mick looked up at him and shook his head from side to side. "Jeff, Jeff, Jeff! I just love you so, but you are such a babe in the woods. What do you think Freemasonry is if it isn't a pagan religion that takes away from the glory of our own Lord, Jesus?"

"Mick, you don't even know what you're talking about," the young man shot back defensively.

"Don't I now? Jeff, I was a Master Mason before you were even born!" he spat out. "I spent 30 years in the Craft and I have been up every leg of the thing and then some. I even dallied in the Islamic ends of it in the Mideast and the Hindu underbelly of it when I served in India. And I am telling you from deep personal involvement that it is *accursed of God* and so is any man who bows his knee at its altar."

He looked at the shocked expression frozen on the face of his friend and softened. "Oh, Jeff, what can I say to you? They came after you like you were a piece of prize candy. It's my own fault for not sitting down with you before they made their move on you. Come on and walk along with me a while," he said as he started down the street again.

"After 30 years of darkness, seeking to lift my own self up into the heavens by my own power, I found out that God sent His own dear Son down from those heavens to find me and set me free from my sins. It's when I gave my life to Jesus that it all became so clear. *He* was the giver of true life, of true peace, and not those things I did in secret. I had to choose between the exaltation I sought within the highest levels of the Craft or exalting the true King. I chose Jesus."

"I didn't do *anything* last night to compromise my love for the Lord or my full and total commitment to Jesus, Mick," Jeff protested.

"Yes, you did, Jeff, and I think you know it already. You fell for one of the oldest tricks in the book, lad," he responded with a forlorn smile. "To start with, you sought the approval of men instead of the approval of God. You let those men praise you right into their snare. Add to that, you swore a blood oath upon your head last night, which is expressly forbidden by the Lord! Even a man who has a Master's of Divinity degree should know that!"

"Mick, it was a simple, harmless thing, not to be taken seriously by anyone," Jeff answered.

"Look, Jeff, you are hardly an expert on Freemasonry after your quick trip through the Stations of the Lodge last night. What you experienced was absolutely the mildest stuff that exists behind the Lodge doors. They wanted to entrap you there, not frighten you away. And yet," he repeated with passion, "you, a minister of the gospel of Christ, swore an oath upon your very own head."

As Jeff began to raise his hand in protest, the elder man pressed on. "Don't you read your Bible? Listen to what Jesus said about your business last night. *'Ye have heard that it hath been said by them of old time, Thou shalt not forswear thyself, but shalt perform unto the Lord thine oaths. But I say unto you, Swear not at all, neither by heaven, for it is God's throne, nor by the earth, for it is his footstool; neither by Jerusalem, for it is the city of the great King. Neither shalt thou swear by thy head, because thou canst not make one hair white or black. Let your communication be Yea, yea; Nay, nay: for whatsoever is more than these cometh of evil.'* Check that out in your Bible, Jeff! They're the very words of Jesus Himself, in Matthew 5:33-37."

They had stopped walking now and stood uncomfortably in front of the cafe. Jeff was silent for awhile, staring over Mick's head toward the mountains to the west. He did not look happy. "I will look at it when I get home, Mick. But I can't believe these men would *knowingly* lead me into *anything* that would be displeasing to the Lord. I'm sorry I've offended you, though, and I hope we can work through this, Mick," he answered with obvious emotion.

"Well, I guess I need to go home and pray about where my wife and I will now attend church. It was bad enough with so many Masons in the place, but with you in the pulpit, there was hope, Jeff," Mick answered. "Can we pray about this right now?" he asked.

As Jeff reluctantly nodded, Mick gripped him tightly by both hands. "Lord God," he prayed, "please open Jeff's eyes to the darkness that has come upon him and our church. Help him to see Your position on this business of Freemasonry and get his feet back on the path You have placed before him. In Christ's name we pray. Amen! Let me hear you say Amen, Jeff," he demanded.

"Amen, Amen!" Jeff responded tensely. "I want only the best the Lord has for me, Mick, and if this stuff with the Lodge is not His best, then I guess I'll have to do something about it. But let the Lord deal with me, Mick, and relax a little, will you?" he asked his friend as he hurried away for home, not even stopping at Tiny's.

"Jeff," Mick called after him, "I love you, brother."

Jeff kept the confrontation with Mick to himself, but he did review the Scripture that Mick had quoted and spent some quality time on his knees before church the next morning. Church was something else again. It's like there are two churches here today, Jeff thought to himself as he walked over from the Education Building to the sanctuary. Maybe it's just that I'm still jumpy over what Mick said, but it seems like part of the church is all smiles today about what happened Friday night, but another whole group seems to be pretty tight-lipped. Jeff sighed and told himself to close his mind to the issue, to put it aside and set his mind on something he could do something about: the ministry today.

As he stood behind the pulpit, it was hard to concentrate on the message. Roy and Ruth Wallace were sitting on one side of the aisle, smiling brightly, while Betty and Mick Sterling sat just a few rows behind them like stone statues. Across the sanctuary the scene was repeated a dozen times. His eyes came to rest on Win and Sue Johnson. Jeff could see Win's jaw muscles moving, as though he were grinding his teeth. It's going to be a long day, he reflected.

Jennifer came up immediately after the end of the service with Mrs. Claudy, who had come to church alone. "Jeff, please take a moment and pray with Sister Claudy for Ray. He's not feeling well today," she said as she took the white-haired lady's tiny hand and placed it tenderly in her husband's giant one. Jeff gratefully spent the next five minutes talking and praying with great zeal for the well-being of Raymond Claudy, looking cautiously every few moments at the dwindling membership heading for the door and their cars.

"Jeff, what on earth was wrong with you today?" Jenny asked over lunch. "Honestly, honey, you got lost a half-dozen times in 30 minutes!" Jennifer leaned back and laughed as he blushed over her commentary on his preaching.

"I don't know, Jen. Something's not feeling right about this Lodge stuff. Half the congregation was pounding me on the back, congratulating me, and the other half of them were giving me the evil eye today."

"Oh, Jeff, that's nonsense. Why on earth would anyone care if you were a Mason or not?"

"I don't know, Jen. It's just some things that Mick told me yesterday."

"Well, there is one thing that I know and it's that you've said *I don't know* over a dozen times today. I think it's time you give it a rest and finish your lunch." Jenny leaned over and squeezed his arm as she reached to kiss his cheek.

Jeff sighed deeply and gave his wife a little disdainful smile as he bent to the task of finishing his lunch. Jenny beamed with amusement as she carried her plate to the sink, sidestepping Moses as he happily entwined himself around her legs.

———————◆———————

By the Wednesday night's midweek service, things seemed to have mellowed out. Jeff was pleased to see Betty and Mick back at the altar that morning praying for several hours. He had gone in with them and shared some of the prayer needs that had come in, especially regarding one of the church members, Raymond Claudy. He had been taken to the hospital in Dillon and was going through a series of tests today and tomorrow. Mick was back to his usual jovial self, and they laughed over a few bits of town gossip. When they left, Jeff felt the first real peace since Mick had confronted him on Saturday morning.

As the meetings broke up for the night, Steve Hanson stepped into Jeff's office, where he was putting away his teaching notes, to discuss the announcements and church bulletin items that were needed for the upcoming Royal Ambassador Week.

Steve elaborated on the full week of programs scheduled, starting with the Royal Ambassador youth taking over the Sunday evening service. There was to be a churchwide spaghetti feed before church on Wednesday, prepared by Steve and the group counselors, with displays set up so the church members could look over some of the projects they had done during the past year. The main portion of the midweek service was to be an awards-and-recognition ceremony for both the boys and their leaders.

"The final event of the week will be the overnight Friday night, Jeff. It would sure be great if you could stay with us for that," Steve cheerfully announced. "That will end with the work party at the church on Saturday morning after the pancake breakfast the boys are going to put together for the men's group. That way you should have at least 40 people to get some of the bigger cleanup jobs out of the way."

"Well, I'm ready," Jeff responded, happily waving a sheet of paper from his desk that contained a list of work he needed done around the place. "If I can just get some help replacing some of those high-up light bulbs in the sanctuary I'll be thrilled and some of the people may actually be able to read their hymnals."

"By the way, Jeff, would it be all right to use several of the basement rooms on Thursday night?" Steve asked as they prepared to leave the room. "We usually use them for our initiation ceremonies for the Lads, Crusaders, and Pioneers."

"I see no problem, Steve," he responded, hitting the lights and closing the door behind him. "I'm looking forward to being there with you. I hear you have the largest initiation group in years."

"We sure do, thanks to having a much larger congregation to draw from since you became our pastor," Steve replied as they went out the side door into the cold night air.

———————◆———————

Steve waited as the room began to fill with the young boys and their fathers. He picked up the instruction book entitled, *Royal Ambassador Ceremonies, Dramas and Recognitions* and scanned through its familiar pages. Its title page stated, *"Copyrighted in 1988 and published by the Brotherhood Commission, SBC, 1548 Poplar Ave., Memphis TN 38104-2493, James H. Smith, President, A Southern Baptist Convention agency supported through the Cooperative Program."* It was a ritual book for Recognition Services and the Initiation Ceremonies of the young men and boys' groups in the Southern Baptist Church. Steve had used it for the several years he had handled the initiation ceremonies and was pleased with the impact it had on the young men. The manual was specifically created for use with the Royal Ambassador program.

Steve enjoyed his role as its leader. He knew that the Royal Ambassador program was part of a strong foundational program to raise up young men to be servants of God and true ambassadors for Christ. Throughout the pages of the ritual manual the name of Christ was lifted up, and Jesus was an obvious and integral part of the entire program. The motto itself, "We are Ambassadors for Christ," came from 2 Corinthians 5:20.

He was surprised, however, to learn that just as every step along the ladder of the Royal Ambassador advancement was filled with deeper commitment to the cause of Christ, each step was equally filled with Masonic ritual, terminology, and metaphor.

His eyes fell to the Recognition Ceremonies on page 8, where the young initiates are told, "Royal Ambassadors, keep this in mind. The shields, badges and other awards that are about to be presented to you are not prizes. These are *tokens* of what you have done or where you have been." Steve knew that the tone of the charges, the way the sentences were formed and spoken, and the use of words such as *token*, *well done*, *travel*, and *journey* were key Masonic words that were more than just subliminal here.

He glanced up the column at another example described in the instructions for the Lads: "You have just begun the *journey* to the mountain of adventure..." and gazed across the page to the instruction for the Trail Blazers on page 9: "*Well done*. You have *advanced* more than halfway up the *mountain of adventure*. Your *token* is in the form of a *shield* with a gold circle around it." And on it goes, he reflected.

When he had discussed this phenomenon with Roy Wallace, the older man had smiled knowingly. "You have to realize, Steve, that these young men are being prepared to be *comfortable* with this kind of ritual, so that when they are later encouraged to step into the mysteries of Freemasonry they will feel on familiar ground. What a blessing!

"As each of those young men stands at the Lodge door, with a hoodwink over his eyes, a cabletow around his neck, and his sleeve and pant leg rolled back, embarking on the mystical journey for higher knowledge and seeking the light of the Lodge, he is going to think, 'Well, it can't be too strange. I did almost this same thing at church when I was in Royal Ambassadors. It must be okay," Roy finished with a satisfied sigh.

Steve was encouraged by the obvious foresight of it all. In looking into these rituals with our understanding of the Masonic forces at work, he thought, these ceremonies appear to have been purposely established by this Brotherhood Commission to prepare young men for that higher initiation into the mysteries of Freemasonry.

Everyone was now set for the initiation, and the boys, their fathers, the counselors, and Jeff were waiting for him to begin the ceremonies.

Jeff sat with Win Johnson, who had a son going through the initiation tonight, and with some of the older boys and other dads in the rear of the center room as Steve went through the "Dubbing of the Swords Ceremony" for the Crusaders. It basically revolved around a Royal Ambassador flag draped over a table in the middle of the room with five white candle-holders placed around the shield in the flag. In the center of the shield was a single lighted red candle which was already lit. As Steve began the service, the single light from just above the table was dimmed.

Jeff felt ill-at-ease as the service continued. Trying to put his finger on his uneasiness, he suddenly recalled the altar at which he knelt in the Lodge just two weeks before, and he wondered if the other Masons in the room realized the similarity in the room setup and furniture. After the Dubbing Ceremony he was asked as pastor to close in prayer, and there followed a short break while the counselors prepared for what Steve had told him was called the Initiation Door Ceremony.

The Door Ceremony began with the young initiates being led to a side preparation room by one of the counselors. Steve, with one of the dads and Tom Adams, the usher who worked with Charlie Miller, stayed inside the room.

After some moments of quiet, there were two sharp knocks on the door. Tom Adams walked to the door and knocked once loudly from the inside. Another single rap came from outside. "Who comes here?" Tom shouted, opening the door and rapping the young man standing there on the left shoulder.

Jeff inhaled sharply as he noticed that it was the young Johnson boy, Joshua, and he was blindfolded, with his right shoe and jacket removed and his left sleeve rolled up. My Lord! Jeff cried out in his mind. This is exactly what I went through at the door in the Lodge and Josh is dressed almost like I was in the Masonic ritual for Entered Apprentice! All that's missing is the cabletow. He felt Win Johnson stirring uneasily at his side.

One of the counselors from the other room was standing with the youngster and spoke. "Mr. Joshua Johnson, a weary traveler along life's highway, seeking entrance and companionship along his journey up the straight and narrow path."

Parts of the Masonic ritual flashed through Jeff's mind. *"A poor blind candidate, who is desirous of being brought from darkness to light and receiving part of the rights, lights, and benefits of this worshipful Lodge, erected to God and dedicated to the Holy Saints John, as many a brother and fellow has done before him."*

Tom Adams addressed the boy. "Mr. Joshua Johnson, is it your free will and desire that you be allowed to enter into our midst?"

Again, Jeff recalled the words he had heard that night. *"Is it of your own free will and accord?"*

Joshua spoke ever so softly. "Yes, it is, sir."

"Have you the key with which to enter?" Tom Adams demanded.

Again, the other counselor answered. "He has it not, but I give it for him." Stepping forward, he clasped Tom's hand and said in a low voice, "Share the light of the world."

Jeff, who had just spent a few hours with Steve the day before working on the memory portion of the degree work in preparation for his own step up into the Second Degree next month, recognized the words again. *"Has he the pass?"* to which the Steward replies, *"He has not. I have it for him." "Give me the pass,"* the Senior Deacon states. *The Steward gives the pass or key to the Senior Deacon in a whisper, "Boaz."*

Jeff came to rigid attention as he watched this ritual unfold, realizing now that the whole thing was wrapped around the Masonic ritual. His eyes locked on those of Win Johnson for a moment as the father searched Jeff's face for some sign of understanding. He could see that Jeff was deeply shocked.

Tom had just responded, "Wait until I return. I shall inform our counselor of your wish," and had walked briskly to the front of the room and was now addressing Steve Hanson. "There is a weary traveler outside our gate, seeking entrance."

Steve responded solemnly, "Let him be escorted in."

Tom returned to the door and addressed the two standing there. "You have permission to enter."

The counselor slowly led the boy in and walked him blindfolded slumberously around the room. Steve rapped his gavel once loudly as they approached each of the four posts. As the youngster passed each post, Steve or the counselor at the post read a portion of Scripture. Jeff recognized Romans 12:1,2, Matthew 10:39, and Luke 14:23, in that order.

Jeff remembered back to the Friday before last. *There were four posts in the Lodge room too! They walked me around them blindfolded just like this! As I passed each station or post each one gave a loud rap on the floor. As the first rap was given Roy Wallace began to recite the 133rd Psalm, and he was just completing it as I finished the tour around the Lodge.*

This routine, including the rapping at the door, was repeated on a second and third trip around the room, and each post reread his Scripture as the boy passed his post.

On the final round of the tour, the travelers stopped at the third station and the counselor knocked again, as before. "Who comes here?" asked the counselor at the station.

"Mr. Joshua Johnson, a weary traveler seeking guidance and companionship on his journey," came the reply.

"Mr. Joshua Johnson," the counselor at the post responded, "The motto 'Share the Light of the World' is taken from John 8:12, which says, *'Then spake Jesus again to them, saying, I am the light of the world; he that followeth me shall not walk in darkness but shall have the light of life.'* As an Ambassador, do you accept the responsibility of sharing the light of the world?"

As young Josh answered, "Yes, I do," Jeff thought of the portion of his initiation where he learned that the light of the world was really the light of the Lodge or Freemasonry.

Finally Joshua was led to the center of the room, where the Bible was open on the table, with the spotlight from above shining directly on it. Steve Hanson walked over and gently helped the boy kneel on his right knee in front of the Bible.

Jeff was reminded that he had been instructed to advance to the altar, too. *"Kneel on your naked left knee; place your right as to form a square, your body erect, your naked left hand supporting the Holy Bible, Square, and Compasses, your naked right hand resting thereon."*

"The Royal Ambassador Pledge," Steve said quietly, "emphasizes the basic purposes of the Royal Ambassador program. If you agree to willingly subscribe to this pledge, please repeat after me."

"As a Royal Ambassador, I will do my best: To become a well-informed responsible follower of

Christ; to have a Christlike concern for all people; to learn how the message of Christ is carried around the world; to work with others in sharing Christ; and to keep myself clean and healthy in mind and body." As Steve led the young man through the pledge, Jeff listened carefully, trying unsuccessfully to detect any hidden signals. You can't find fault with any of that, he chided himself.

Steve reached over, picked up the Bible, and handed it to the counselor who had led the boy in. He held the Bible in front of the boy. Steve leaned over the youngster. "To seal this pledge, you will place your right hand on the Bible." He turned to Tom Adams. "Please remove the blindfold so that Joshua can see the Bible. This is the key which opens the door to our fellowship so that we may work together in being Ambassadors for Christ." At the moment the blindfold was pulled away, someone hit the light switch and the room was bathed in light.

Jeff could see that they were applying the same effects as he remembered from the Lodge, where the design of both darkened rooms was such that a single light would shine just at this moment upon the Bible. In both the Lodge and the Royal Ambassador rituals, the attention of the candidate is directed to the Bible, while some kind of oathtaking was being conducted.

Steve turned back to the boy. "I hold in my hand the membership pin. This shield stands for faith and indicates that the life and teachings of Jesus Christ guide the wearer in his daily life. Do you promise to share the light of the world as you wear this membership pin?" he asked the kneeling child.

"I do," replied Josh firmly.

Steve helped the boy up and fastened the pin to Joshua's shirt. He then turned to those in attendance. "Members, join with me in extending Joshua the handclasp of welcome into our midst."

Jeff sighed his great relief that they hadn't asked Joshua to swear an oath such as he had had to swear. Maybe I'm just too jumpy, he thought, but Jeff knew that something was terribly out of balance.

Eleven more times the group went through the same ritual, before the entire group of initiates were processed through the system. Jeff left the basement worn out beyond measure. At the top of the stairs Win Johnson was waiting while his son was digging a jacket out of the pile near the door. "Do you agree with what went on down there, Jeff?" he asked.

"No, I don't, Win," Jeff answered with a sinking feeling, knowing that Win was distraught. "I'm going to have to talk with Steve about this. It wasn't what I expected, and no boy is ever going to be blindfolded again in a church where I am pastor."

"Well, thank God for that!" Win shot back. "Jeff, I warned you about the 'Inner Circle' here. You are fast becoming a part of the problem rather than a part of the solution. You better figure out whether you are a man of God or a man of the Lodge." With that he turned and walked out the door into the night. Jeff stood there for a long time staring at the door, realizing that he had a significant problem on his hands. Sighing again deeply, he turned back to the job of trying to close up the place for the night.

CHAPTER FIVE

He worked his way down the stairs, saying good-bye with a cheerfulness that he really didn't feel to the young men and their dads coming up from the basement. Steve was at the far end of the long room talking quietly to Tom Adams and several others. Jeff was surprised to see his father-in-law and was at a loss to remember when he had slipped in. As tired as Jeff was, he knew that he had to make some sort of protest to Steve over the mystery ceremonies he had just witnessed.

"Steve, can I see you for a second?" he asked as he interrupted them, greeting Roy Wallace with a quick handshake and nod. Steve left the others and walked to the center of the room with Jeff.

"Outstanding initiation, Jeff," Steve said. He smiled enthusiastically with excitement in his eyes. "It was the best I've ever seen here."

Jeff knew to be careful with his friend and spoke cautiously. "Steve, I'm truly thrilled to see such a team of men and boys working together in the Royal Ambassadors, but don't you think the ceremony was a bit too Masonic for a simple church group?"

Steve searched Jeff's face for a minute and saw the concern there. "Jeff, that was the official Southern Baptist Ceremonies manual. Word for word! Don't read something into it that isn't there."

"You have been given a special look into the path of further light," he continued quietly, trying to keep the conversation private in spite of the presence of others. "You see things that the average person misses entirely and that's the beauty of the Craft. Years from now, a light bulb will go off for a few of the boys who were here tonight and some

129

things will fall into place. If they never petition a Lodge, what happened here will never mean a single thing more than what it did right here." He smiled warmly and looked up at this young pastor.

"Jeff, we still have another Ritual to do tonight for Tom Day's son and two other boys. It's called the Bishop Initiation for Pioneers, and while it's supposed to be very special and pretty secret, it is right out of the manual, word for word. Maybe you should head on home and let Roy and me handle it alone."

Jeff glanced at the others who were waiting on Steve. They were watching anxiously as the two were speaking. Jeff told himself to drop it for the time being and get out of there. This wasn't the time or place to deal with it. "Can we talk about this sometime next week, when we have some time, Steve?" he asked.

"Sure, Jeff, and here," he said as he handed Jeff several sheets of paper stapled together. "This is a photocopy of the Bishop Initiation. Read it over and we'll talk about it then. Okay?" he asked.

Jeff thanked him for the papers and released him back to the others. "Go ahead with your plans. I'm heading home for the night. I'm so exhausted I can barely keep my eyes open." Moments later he was out the door and hurrying across the lawn to the parsonage.

Jeff sat at his bedside reading the several sheets of instruction for the ceremonies now taking place in the church basement. He slowly turned the pages as he absorbed the details of the ritual.

"Listen to this, Jen," he spoke in frustration to his sleepy wife. "This manual tells them to hold this initiation of the Pioneer boys in secret, and they blindfold the kids and run them through some kind of Masonic ritual even heavier than I went through."

"Well, I don't think that's right, Jeff, do you?" she responded as she sat up. "Did they get your permission to do that? Did they ask each of the boys' parents if it was okay to do it?"

"I seriously doubt that they talked to every parent, but one of the leaders, Tom Adams, has a son going through it." He sighed in obvious distress. "I'm afraid they did get my permission to do the initiations, but I had no idea that this kind of thing was going to be done in a church boys' group, right there in our own church."

"I'm not trying to tell you what to do, honey, but it seems to me that you might want to talk to my dad about it. I'm sure he can help you get it straightened out."

"Nice thought, Jenny," he answered. "But your dad is over there right now doing the secret ceremony with them." Jennifer looked at her husband and threw up her hands and flopped back on the bed dramatically.

"I tell you what I *will* do, though, and that's go over it with someone I think can help me." Jeff reached for the phone on the bedstand and called Mick Sterling.

Chapter
6

It was early the next morning when Mick came in and sat with Jeff in his office at the church. Jeff picked up the papers that Steve had given him and read the title. "This is the section they call THE BISHOP INITIATION."

He handed some papers to Mick. "I made a copy of my copy for you to look at. This ceremony is specifically designed for Pioneers," he said. "It must be set up with an air of secrecy and has even more direct ties to Freemasonry than the one I sat through last night, Mick. These are the instructions detailed on pages 26-28 of the Brotherhood Manual I told you about.

"What bothered me about it was that in it the Counselor is explicitly instructed to be secretive in the operation of the ritual. Here, let me read it to you," he said as he scanned the data on the first page. " 'It is suggested that this initiation service be known only to you, a few selected leaders, parents and those boys who have been initiated. This initiation is a reprint of an emphasis incorporated some years ago by Ivyloy Bishop, the first national director of the Royal Ambassador program.'

"You can see from the picture of the initiation room on page 27 that the room is prepared with a series of piles with cans, bricks, rocks, sticks and a ladder. Next to the ladder is a table with a Bible on it."

Jeff paused for a moment as he studied the picture further. "Now I know why they wanted to use the church basement: It has a second room opening up into the ritual room just like in the Manual. Each boy is taken to this side room by the Director, where his coat is removed, his sleeves are rolled up, and he is blindfolded, just like they did to me at the Lodge. He is then led to the door of the ritual room. Do you see the parallel?" He looked up at Mick for a quick sign of understanding. As Mick nodded, Jeff's gaze returned to the page.

"Let me go through the ceremony for you , Mick, and then I've got a few questions to ask you," Jeff said. He began to read again from the manual. " 'The Director gives the secret knocks, which are: two quick raps, pause, then two more quick knocks. The Counselor [inside] answers with the same knock, opens the door, asks who the candidate is, if he will keep the secrets, do the work and bear the responsibilities of a Royal Ambassador. After the candidate answers "yes," he is admitted.

" 'After he is admitted he is told that he is going on a journey and must pray for guidance. After a short prayer, *the candidate is given a heavy sack of bricks or rocks. It should be about all he can carry to symbolize a real burden.*

" 'Carrying the burden, the candidate is led two or three times around the room. . . . At the end of the last round he is rudely halted by the Counselor . . . (removes the burden). The candidate is then walked rapidly forward. . . . A stick is held across his path in such a way that it lightly taps him on the forehead. He is told that this is to teach him that if on the journey of life he is proud and high-headed and does not bow humbly to the will of God, he will meet with obstacles. He is told to bow very low, and so passes under the rod. . . .' "

Jeff paused for a moment, leaning back in his chair. "I just can't believe this is something that went on in our church basement last night." With a deep sigh he returned to the pages of the material on the desk.

" 'He is now marched over various rough objects in his path. These may include tin cans, bricks, a ladder lying flat on the floor, stairs, etc. All this time the Director is holding him by the arm to prevent him from falling down, but allowing the candidate to stumble along.

" 'The candidate is halted and told that the path of life is not always easy, but is often rough and difficult to travel. He will find pitfalls and stumbling blocks along the way. He will not be able to see what is ahead, but if he with faith puts his hand in the hand of Christ as he did with the Director, he will be helped along the way.

" 'The candidate is led to the ladder and similar analogy is used as he climbs the ladder being held by several of the men.

" 'The candidate is now conducted to a low table or chair on which lies an open Bible. The candidate kneels before

this Bible; his right hand is placed over his heart and his left hand rests on the edge of the table touching the Bible. The candidate is told that he is kneeling before an open Bible and that his right hand is over his heart as a symbol of sincerity. He is instructed that in this position he is to take the obligation of his chapter and if he will promise to keep the obligation, he is to answer I do after each of [a series of] questions.'"

Jeff continued as Mick listened with great intent. *" 'Following the obligation, which deals with Christian lifestyle, the room is made entirely dark. The Counselor turns a flashlight on the Bible. With the candidate still kneeling, the blindfold is taken off and he is told that the world is in darkness without the Bible; that the Scriptures are God's light that comes from above.... The lights are turned on and the candidate is greeted by each member of the Chapter. This ritual is repeated for each initiate.'"*

Jeff was clearly dismayed. "I know that the Bible and Christ are used in the ritual here, Mick, but the parallels and tie-in to Freemasonry are *astonishing!* First we have the Masonic blindfolding, the sleeves rolled up, and the secret raps and signals at the entry door between two ritual workers. The Brotherhood manual clearly instructs that the candidate must be asked if he is willing to *'keep the secrets.'* This is asked *prior* to the young man's knowledge of any of the details of those secrets."

"Don't you see the design and purpose of that?" Mick interrupted. "He must blindly trust his Royal Ambassador leaders, just as he will be asked in later life in Freemasonry to trust the Worshipful Master. Of course, I personally have seen that the Worshipful Master *will* lie to an Entered Apprentice so that

he is seduced into swearing the Masonic Obligation, but that's another story," the older man said.

"You notice here, Jeff, that in the Pioneer ritual,
the oath is also referred to as *'the obligation of the
Chapter,'* just as it is in the Lodge. You are absolutely
right about the candidate being asked to promise to
keep the obligation without any knowledge of the
actual extent of that obligation. It's an occult trap!
Here it is pretty simple and deals only with the
young man's relationship with Christ. However,
Christ Himself would never demand such an oath
from a single soul on earth. So, just as it does in
Freemasonry, it binds the candidate to occult principles."

Mick settled down in his chair and began to discuss the ritual with the apprehensive pastor. "Jeff,
the reason the warning flags flew for you is that you
saw that the bait-and-switch method of occult
indoctrination was clearly present here. You are a
pretty smart fellow, but you fell for it yourself—
hook, line, and sinker! What chance did those boys
have last night? None!

"Why is it necessary to blindfold and lead these
young men around some form of a Lodge room?
Why are Christian leaders asking young men to
violate scriptural warnings and swear these oaths of
obligation? I truly believe it is to soften their spiritual sensitivities for the actual rites of the higher
degrees of Freemasonry. It's a blasted Masonic trap
right in the middle of the Christian church itself!"
he shouted as he pounded his fist into the side arm
of his chair.

After he calmed down a bit, Mick leaned intently toward a grim, white-faced Jeff. "Let me tell you a few things that are going on here that you can't see yet from your limited view of the Lodge rituals. In the higher Masonic rituals, I recognize several *very* close parallels to the Pioneer initiation. Perhaps the easiest to understand is the Royal Arch or Seventh Degree ritual in what is called the Christian or the York Rite. This is the degree in which the candidate steps directly into the occult path of gnostic, mystical enlightenment. Here he learns the secret name of the Masonic god and takes upon himself the password of the Royal Arch member, *I AM THAT I AM*.

"Candidates for that degree are presented in groups of threes, and it always requires that same number of Royal Arch Masons to pronounce the sacred name. The name is 'JAOBULON,' Jeff. 'JAO' is the Greek word for 'JEHOVAH,' 'BUL' is a rendering of the name 'BAAL,' and 'ON' is the name used in the Babylonian mysteries to call upon the name of their evil deity, 'OSIRIS'!"

Jeff was white-faced as Mick continued. "What you see here, as the god of Freemasonry, is a three-headed monster so remote from the Christian God of the Holy Trinity and so blasphemous that it would damn the eternal soul of anyone who would dare to pronounce its name in any ritual of worship. Do you wonder why I was so upset at you the other morning?" Jeff just shook his head from side to side as the horror of Mick's revelation set in. It was a long minute before Mick picked up where he left off.

"Let's see," he pondered. "I guess I was talking about the Royal Arch Degree work and its comparison to the Pioneer ritual. The Royal Arch candidates are prepared by having their coats removed, blindfolds placed over their eyes, and being tied together with a long rope, with about three feet of slack between them. Sound familiar?" he asked with a sardonic smile.

"The candidates are presented as three sojourners from Babylon. A Royal Arch member plays the role of the Principal Sojourner, who leads them by the rope. Once past the entry door and the usual knocking or rapping and passwords, he speaks these words to the candidates." Mick smiled again. "Bear in mind, Jeff, that I was once heavily involved in this stuff before I repented. So forgive me if I still remember the memory work of the upper degrees. Maybe the Lord let me retain it for this very purpose. *'Companions, you will follow me. I will bring the blind by a way they know not; I will lead them in paths they have not known; I will make darkness light before them, and crooked things straight. These things will I do unto them, and will not forsake them. Stoop low, brethren, he that humbleth himself shall be exalted.'*"

He sighed and drew in a deep breath. "Meanwhile, Lodge members form two facing lines and interlock their fingers, forming a low arch under which the candidates must stoop and under which they are eventually forced to the floor to crawl their way through. This is a direct counterpart to the Pioneer ritual of stooping under the stick to *'bow very low.'*

"Notice the similarity between the Pioneer Director and the Principal Sojourner. Both are there to lead the blindfolded candidates through the perils of darkness and trials and bring them to the light. While the Director is portrayed as the example of Christ, the Principal Sojourner is not hampered by any such restriction. He and the Lodge represent the *real* light, the truth, and the way. Jesus is not mentioned."

Mick stood and leaned over the desk, intent on making his point. "Both rituals require the same form of solemn obligation and both ask its candidates to agree to the ritual and obligation in *advance* of any bit of knowledge and by virtue of some implied but absent free will. Both use the metaphor of darkness and light and both recognize the leader and group as the truth-bearers. Both require the candidates to kneel before a Bible to take their *obligation*. I tell you, Jeff, they are both cut out of the same cloth. These things are not created by the mind of Christ. How could they be?" he asked, his voice raised in frustration. "They come from the mind of the devil himself, I tell you!"

He fell back into his seat and picked up the papers again. "Let's get back to the comparisons. In the Royal Arch Degree, the three candidates are led around the Lodge room just as they are in the Pioneer initiation. Each of the candidates shoulders a heavy sack supposed to be his working tools and follows the Principal Sojourner, going single-file to a corner of the room where a quantity of blocks or bricks are scattered around. The candidates find a trap door, and after returning to the High Priest of the Chapter to report their find, one of them eventually goes down into a lower chamber to first recover three small symbolic objects. In this ritual, a ladder is usually used.

"In the obligation of this Degree," he continued, "the candidate swears a lengthy oath of very severe proportions. In part, he states, '*I furthermore promise and swear that I will keep all the secrets of a Companion Royal Arch Mason when communicated to me as such, or I knowing them to be such, without exceptions.*' At the conclusion of this three-page oath, the initiate is commanded to seal his oath by kissing the Bible or other sacred book seven times."

Mick shook his head sadly. "One must wonder what dark secrets have been hidden from the world of truth and justice under this foolish guise of such fraternal fidelity."

"Mick, is this the basis for the Ambassador ritual?" Jeff probed.

"Well, I'd like to say it's only that deep," he responded, "but I'm sad to say that it's just the tip of the iceberg. The blasted stuff also comes out of the initiation ritual of the Shrine. The official name is The Ancient Arabic Order, Nobles of the Mystic Shrine, and it is one Masonic group that openly mocks the dignity of any sort of Christian integrity. The initiation ritual is designed with numerous sexual overtones, and it is hard to imagine that any decent man would want his wife or children to ever watch him perform it.

"In one of the least offensive parts of the Shriner ritual, I can recall another extremely close connection to the Royal Ambassador initiation. As in every one of the rituals, the candidates are hoodwinked and in stocking feet enter after three loud alarms are sounded. At first they proceed one-by-one on carpet, then upon a spread of corn husks, then an area strewn with pebbles, followed by a ladder with close rounds, and chairs folded and laid down or any rough road laid out through the hallways or rooms used."

"I know I sound like a broken record, Mick, but I'm still shocked that there is such a specific tie-in between the two," Jeff broke in as the older man finished his comparison.

"Let me repeat myself also," Mick responded strongly. "We must realize that these young men going through the Bishop Initiation are being prepared to accept spiritual submission to the inner depths of Freemasonry without them having any spiritual warning bells ringing. Freemasonry will have a *familiar spirit*. It will bring to the surface those good feelings they had last night when they received the acceptance and approval of those in authority over them and from those they love. The only thing that could have more strongly bound them to the demonic power of Freemasonry would have been for you to have been part of their initiation. I thank God that you pulled out in time last night."

"Mick, I can't thank you enough for all your help and insight in all this. I've been a real fool and need to sort a lot of things out before I go and make any more of a fool out of myself," Jeff said as he reached for the phone ringing on his desk.

It was Jennifer. "Hi, sweetheart," he responded.

CHAPTER SIX

"Jeff," she said, her voice strained and urgent, "Sister Claudy called me. Her husband has taken a real turn for the worse. She's at the hospital in Dillon and doesn't think he's going to make it. Hurry home, sweetheart! We need to get down there right away!" she cried.

———————◆———————

Jeff guessed that the entire town had shown up for the funeral. The sanctuary was filled with flower arrangements, and the somber friends and family of Ray Claudy came and sat in silence as the music from the organist softly drew them in from the outside, where the bright, sunny day had given an uplift to the thoughts of Ray Claudy's homegoing to heaven. There are always mixed feelings at such times, Jeff thought. We are surely glad the suffering is over, but the loss leaves an empty place in our hearts.

The coffin lay below the pulpit in the center of the altar area, and on the front row to either side sat the Claudy family, their children, and the fidgeting grandchildren. The service had been uplifting and a blessing to the gathering of family and friends. As Jeff finished his remarks, the organist began an extended rendition of "Rock of Ages" with well-practiced hands gliding across the keys. There was something of an inner sigh from the family as the peaceful promise of heaven's reality filled their hearts as this time of sorrowful goodbye came to an end.

Jenny caught Jeff's eye and smiled her little "I'm proud of you" smile. She was pleased at his gentle handling of this, his first funeral. They had been with the Claudys almost continuously since they raced to the hospital. That long night, as Ray slipped away, Jeff proved to her once again that he had the anointing of the Lord in his pastoral ministry to these people. Perhaps things will get back in perspective again, she thought.

Suddenly she felt something heavy come upon the place, something dark. She turned to face the source of this dire thing and saw a group of somber men coming into the back of the chapel from the side room. Her father was in the forefront. She spun to look at Jeff. His face was drained and he looked like he was literally going to get up and bolt from the place. With deathlike ashen faces, the group marched in procession up the center aisle as though in some medieval trance. Jennifer barely breathed as she watched.

They were some of the older men from the Masonic Lodge, dressed in dark lifeless clothes, black ties, and white gloves. Some wore white aprons and others wore aprons with fringes and figures within them. All wore black arm bands and green evergreen sprigs on their breasts. Her father carried something that appeared to be a Bible, while several others carried rods or batons with black-and-white ribbons tied to them.

Jeff felt physically ill and pushed back into his chair as though to get away from the approaching group of men. The somber beat of their steps as they approached the coffin drove away the quiet peace he had experienced during the earlier portion of the funeral, and he sensed a form of spiritual darkness falling upon the congregation. These men have brought an evil, contrary spirit among us, he thought in panic. He and Jenny looked at each other in alarm and both began to pray silently as they watched what ensued.

Rigid in their movements, the Masons gathered around the coffin and chanted the Lord's Prayer in a desolate monotone. Roy Wallace stepped to the head of the casket, then spoke a few words, the understanding of which was obscured by his mumbling recitation. Jeff did remember the words " . . . *the dread messenger of death.*" The fellows on his right and left traded equally bleak and mystic bits of memorized words of mourning. Jeff could catch only brief snatches of the words, such as *"he comes forth as a flower and is cut down . . . man dieth and wasteth away . . . all men shall be judged according to the deeds done in the body . . . the house of mourning, and . . . the gloom of death."*

They continued, as though driven by mechanical control, in a series of mutterings and sprinkling of leaves and their evergreen sprigs over the coffin, upon which they had placed a white apron that symbolized what Roy Wallace murmured was the *"universal dominion of death."*

Declaring the words *"So mote it be"* in deep unison, they turned and marched out in that same sepulchral fashion, leaving the entire congregation in some sort of stunned, hopeless stupor. Jeff saw Betty and Mick stand in the back of the church, their lips moving rapidly as they prayed while the procession marched out past them.

The peace and confidence in heaven that had filled the sanctuary just minutes ago was replaced by a jagged disquiet. Jeff could see that Mrs. Claudy seemed disoriented and fraught with a spirit of depression and despair. He hurried to the pulpit.

"It is so wonderful to know that our brother is already in the presence of the Lord. He went there the moment he closed his eyes. We stand firm in the peace that passes all understanding. Sister Claudy and family, we want to express our deepest sympathy and love to you today. The ladies of the church have prepared food, and we invite you all to visit with the family for a little bit over in the Education Building." He motioned for the ushers to come forward and bring the service to its close.

Chapter
7

Jennifer was sitting quietly at the table when Jeff finally made his way back to the house. He had gone back to the church after their return from the cemetery to be sure everything was in order. She jumped up, poured him a cup of fresh coffee, and waved him into the living room. "Jeff, that funeral thing was something I had never seen as long as I have lived in this town. I don't know a whole lot, but I do know that something was way out of line spiritually there today," she said. She sat on the sofa, inviting him to sit next to her. Moses thought the invitation included him, and Jeff returned the puppy to the floor with firm instructions to stay there.

Jennifer showed deep concern on her face. "Honey," she continued, "if you're having doubts about this Freemasonry thing, why don't you call your dad and talk to him? I just know he'll be able to give you some good advice."

Jeff looked at his wife with wonder. "How do I get myself into these situations?" he lamented. "I talked to half the country about this and never once thought to call my dad and discuss it with him! I'll give him a call later tonight, Jenny, when I know I can get him alone and with a little time to talk."

Jenny beamed at him with approval in her eyes. "Good. It's settled, then! I want to put this stuff behind us and just act like some normal couple for awhile." She reached over and gave him a kiss on the cheek.

———◆———

Jeff sat at his desk in the church office, listening to the phone ring at his folks' house. He could imagine his father reaching for the phone, thinking that the call was from one of his own church members with some special problem. Jeff knew his dad would be surprised that it was his own son. He smiled as he recognized his father's voice on the line. "Hi, dad! Got some time to give an old country preacher some advice?" he asked.

Jeff spent over an hour as he poured out the whole story to his father, pausing now and then to answer specific questions his dad would raise.

"That's it, dad," Jeff said as he concluded with the declaration of his problems. "The biggest question is what do I do now?"

"Jeff, this isn't as difficult as you may think, son." There was a warmth to the voice that almost brought tears of relief to Jeff. "You've never had a problem with deciding right from wrong, nor have you ever hesitated in acting on your decision, and I don't expect you will this time.

"First," his father continued, "I have had to deal with the Masonic problem myself, years ago, just as I imagine every minister has had to. For me the decision was to stay away from it. The reason was simple: Our call in the ministry is to fulfill the evangelical commission of Christ as He gave it in Matthew 24:14, to preach the gospel and prepare for the soon coming of the Lord. Right?" he asked.

"Right!" responded his son.

"Well, simply put, Jeff, that leaves us no choice but to give full, wholehearted devotion to our calling, and it's not too difficult to see that if a man were to be involved with the Masonic Lodge, it would require much of his time and interest and actually take away from the work of the Lord in his life. Right?"

"Right," answered his son. Jeff coupled the answer with a short laugh as he remembered the many instructions he had received throughout his youth with his dad's special *"Right"* system of correction.

"Jeff," his dad continued, "look at the basic problem that Freemasonry has with biblical Christianity. First, its very existence is based on secrecy. It already has you upset because you know what God's Word says about it. In John 18:20 Jesus said that He always spoke and taught openly. In Luke 12:2,3 He said that those things whispered in the ear secretly should be shouted from the rooftops. He seemed to deal with the Masonic ritual in a pretty straightforward manner.

"Next, look at the oaths and binding obligations you were required to swear, Jeff. Again, if Jesus Christ is Lord of your life, then why not just obey Him? He said in Matthew 5: 33-37 that you are not to swear at all—not by heaven or earth or by your own head. Jesus wants you to live a life in which your yes simply and honestly means yes and your no means no. I would imagine that swearing to have your throat slit and your tongue ripped out by its roots would be a violation of that instruction. Right?"

Jeff smiled at the simple truth of his father's statement. "Right, dad! You are absolutely right!" he answered.

"Let's also not forget to whom you made those binding obligations, son. I think it is safe to assume that many of those within even your local Lodge are not born-again Christian brethren. In fact, since the Lodge only requires a belief in *a* god, *any* god, you have more than likely sworn a binding obligation to more than one infidel. Scripture emphatically prohibits you from doing that, Jeff!"

Jeff could hear the rustling of pages as his father looked up a Scripture. He continued. "Let me read you what 2 Corinthians 6:14,15 very clearly states: *'Be ye not unequally yoked together with unbelievers; for what fellowship hath righteousness with unrighteousness? And what communion hath light with darkness? And what concord hath Christ with Belial? Or what part hath he that believeth with an infidel?'* He says in verse 17, *'Wherefore come out from among them and be ye separate, saith the Lord, and touch not the unclean thing; and I will receive you. . . .'*

"Where are you in that list of people, Jeff? Are you a believer or an unbeliever? Are you a reflection of His light or are you darkness? Are you in harmony with Christ or Belial, righteousness or unrighteousness?" His father paused for Jeff's response.

"I'm a believer, dad," he answered. "I'm in harmony with Christ and His righteousness. At least I was until I got mixed up with the Lodge. I'm so sorry, dad." Tears welled up in Jeff's eyes as he saw the magnitude of the sin of Freemasonry.

"Okay, son. I know your heart is pure before the Lord in this. Let me show you just one more thing. The reference to the *'saith the Lord'* portion of 2 Corinthians 6:17 is in Isaiah 52:11. It says very strongly, *'Depart ye, depart ye, go ye out from thence, touch no unclean thing; go ye out of the midst of her; be ye clean, that bear the vessels of the Lord.'* "

His father paused for a moment before continuing. "Now, Jeff, this is talking directly to you. *You* are one of His servants. *You* are one of those who carry the vessels of the Lord. He says to come out from the unclean thing and be pure. Is that what you feel Christ would have you do in the matter, son?"

"Oh, dad! In my heart I know I am out of it already," Jeff cried. "But what about all the harm I've done and will do to so many people in the process? I feel like crawling away from here tonight in the dark!"

"Jeff, the Lord already knows your heart and has your answer. Listen to what verse 12 tells you to do

155

next: *'Ye shall not go out with haste, nor go by flight, for the Lord will go before you, and the God of Israel will be your reward.'* The next verse says that His servant shall *deal prudently* or act wisely, and I'm sure that you will, son."

Jeff felt a wave of relief so strong it was almost physical. "I guess I've been a pretty foolish fellow. There is some personal housecleaning I'm going to have to do. Oh, the trials of youth!" he moaned.

"Don't forget, Jeff, that you need to go out just as publicly as you went in. *You are the pastor there*, and the lay members need to know exactly why you are leaving the Lodge you just joined." He laughed softly. "You remind me so much of Timothy. Paul must have looked on him as a son, just like I do you. He told him in 1 Timothy 4:12, *'Let no man despise thy youth, but be thou an example of the believers in word, in conversation, in charity, in spirit, in faith, in purity.'*

"At the end of that chapter he admonished Timothy to *'take heed unto thyself and unto the doctrine; continue in them, for in doing this thou shalt both save thyself and them that hear thee.'* Those are tough orders in a spot like this, son, but I'm more than confident that you're up to it. Jeff, your mother and I thank the Lord that you are such a mighty man of God!"

———◆———

Jeff and Jennifer talked long into the night as Jeff shared the things he had spoken about with his dad. The young couple knew they were in for a rough time, especially with her father. Jenny sat on the bed next to Jeff and hugged a squirming Moses, cuddling him lovingly.

"You know, Jeff," she said, "I really don't think my mother is so far into this stuff that she won't see your point. I didn't really understand the problem with it until the funeral and what you told me today. Yet here I was in a key position with Job's Daughters. The kicker is going to be my father. He was so proud of you joining the Lodge, and it's going to really upset him, especially now that he's an officer in the State Lodge," she added.

Jeff rose up from his pillow and joined the cuddle. "We're going to have to take a stand with it, Jen," he said. "I want to be as gentle as possible in doing it, but I don't feel like I'm right with the Lord until I openly remove my name from membership and tell our church people why."

"Let's just try to do it without having some major knock-down-drag-out battle with my dad, okay?" she pleaded.

"Sweetheart, you know your dad loves us both enough to understand why I need to back out. I'm sure it can be done with a minimum of problems," he assured her.

Roy Wallace slammed his hand down onto the table with a resounding crash. "How dare you say these things to me in front of my daughter!" he exploded. "You make me sick! I took you in and gave you this pastorate. I handed it to you on a platter so my daughter could be near her mother!"

He rose from his chair, his face contorted and red. He stood, shaking his fist at Jeff. "How dare you spit in my face like this!" he shouted in a rage.

Jennifer's father was *not* happy with the news of Jeff's decision to leave the Lodge. Jennifer and Jeff had asked him to come for lunch so they could talk over the problem, but lunch had lasted only long enough for Jeff to gingerly introduce the subject. Jennifer began to cry and Moses had fled to the sanctuary of the living room, crawling under a corner chair.

"Look, Roy. I think you need to calm down a bit. We aren't talking about the end of the world here. We're talking about a membership in a club, a fraternity," Jeff said as he tried to reason with the angry man.

"Don't *you* try to tell me what Masonry is!" his father-in-law shouted. "Let *me* tell *you* that you don't have the foggiest idea what you're messing with! You straighten up and get your act together before you find yourself and your little wife out in the street!"

"Dad, what are you saying?" cried Jennifer. "How can you say you love us and talk to us that way?" She was on the edge of hysterics as she watched her father in his fury.

Roy calmed down a bit as he saw the frightened look on his daughter's face. "I only wanted what was best for you both. How could Jeff take the hand of fellowship that we extended to him in love and suddenly decide that we are some *evil organization of devil worshipers?*"

"Roy, that's not even fair," Jeff answered. "All I said was that when you brought me into the initiation, you promised that I would be asked to do nothing that would be in conflict with my Christian beliefs, but once I was into the ritual, I was asked to do and say things that I am convinced were *not* of God and *did* conflict with my beliefs."

Roy pointed his finger sharply at the young man. "Well, you did swear those oaths before God, and you better live up to them!" he exclaimed. "And the Bible has lots of examples to support me. King Herod promised Salome anything she wanted and sealed it with an oath before God. Then she asked for the head of John the Baptist, and even though he didn't want to do it, he ordered that her request be granted because his oath was before God. And he swore that oath *before* he knew what it was she was going to ask him!"

"That may be true, Roy, but it's hardly an example of biblical heroics," Jeff answered. "What kept Herod bound by that oath? Was it because he feared God or the crowd of people at his banquet? If he feared God, he would have renounced his oath and repented of it. It seems to me that his pride and his fear of losing his power over the crowd forced him to act against his own better judgment. I have no intention of ever getting to the place where I would compromise my commitment to Christ, especially through some secret ritual and violent oath. I'm sorry, but I fear God more than I fear my reputation in the Lodge."

"Well, fear this, young man!" his father-in-law snapped. "If you do *anything* to embarrass me, this

Lodge, or the Masons in this town, you best be packing your bags because you won't last a day after you do!"

Roy Wallace spun around to face his daughter, who sat in shock, tears streaming down her face. "You better get this guy back in line if you know what's good for you, little lady." Before she could answer, he fled to the kitchen door and hurried outside, slamming the door behind him.

Chapter
8

J eff walked to the pulpit. The sanctuary was filled with the repetition of the refrain from the last hymn as the choir slowly filed out from the loft area behind him. He waited quietly until the sound of the organ ceased and the choir had taken their seats among the congregation. Almost 200 people filled the pews, waiting quietly for their pastor to begin speaking.

"It's so good to see this sanctuary filled to overflowing," Jeff began. "Time sure flies when you're having fun, especially in Montana. It's hard to believe that it has been almost a year now that we have been together. God has been moving mightily in Jenny's and my lives. He moved dramatically just to bring us here to Badger Lake and to this church. While a year isn't a very long time, we have worked together as a pastor and people, and in that time one word has stood out above all others in my own personal Christian walk: *commitment*! Commitment to God and commitment to the people of this congregation, to my family and to this community.

"As God has moved in my life during these past months, and as I have ministered to many of you during some of your problem times, I've been able to see how easy it is for any of us to be deceived and drawn away from our Christian walk. An example of that kind of subtle deception is the celebration of Halloween. It was in October of last year that I shared with you the roots of Halloween and how it was brought into sync with the Christian holiday of All Saints' Day. I shared with you the evil of that celebration, and some of you were very upset and rebuked my words. Some of you learned the truth about that holiday, and some of you were surprised that I would speak out on the subject. A few of you were actually *grateful* that I took the stand that I did. *All of you* were required to react in some way to the word of warning you were given. But it was my responsibility as your pastor to study the Word of God and to bring you godly truth and direction, no matter how difficult it may be at times.

"I'm afraid that today is another one of those difficult times. Except that this time, I'm more of the problem and less of the solution. You see, in spite of all my training and spiritual preparation, in spite of a Master's Degree in Theology and a lifetime of membership in the church, I have made a serious miscalculation: I failed to listen to that quiet whisper of the Holy Spirit that was warning me to be careful of deception."

Jeff paused and took a long, slow breath. "Well, I have to confess that I have allowed myself to fall prey to the sin of seeking to please men more than the Lord. I have allowed myself to be gently deceived, not by enemies, but by well-meaning friends and loved ones. Now I need to bring my own sin before you and expose it to God's truth just as openly and honestly as I did with the subject of Halloween."

Jeff gazed across the faces of the congregation as he watched the effect his words were having. His eyes rested momentarily on those of Roy Wallace, and he saw seething anger buried beneath the rigid exterior of the man. He glanced quickly to the other side of the church where Jennifer was sitting, silent and apprehensive. Her eyes were warm and loving, but even from the pulpit he could see that they were filled to the edge with tears.

The congregation sat in silence, leaning out toward him in expectation of his next words. Mick and Betty Sterling were seated in the rear of the church, but Jeff could see them clearly and knew they were bathing this meeting in silent prayer. Tom Adams and his family were seated with the Johnsons, and Tom's eyes searched his own as he glanced his way.

"Before I begin what is going to be a very difficult subject, I'd like to ask one of our board members, Win Johnson, to pray for me and for our congregation."

Win stood immediately and from his place in the middle of the sanctuary, solemnly lifted up his voice in prayer. "Heavenly Father, we come before Your mighty throne as Your children in and of Your Word, asking that You bless our pastor and bring Your Holy Spirit mightily through him this day in the message that he has for us. Help him to say what You want to be said, and bring that message to this congregation that we may hear and learn in our hearts and our minds, that we may put to use what we hear this day. Move by Your Holy Spirit this very morning that we may be strengthened, O Lord. I ask it all in Jesus' name, Amen."

"Thank you, Win," Jeff said as Win returned to his seat. "It's not going to be easy for me to share with you today," he continued, "for I guess I care what you might think of me and my spiritual maturity. Many of you will wonder how I could be so foolish. I've already shared this with a few others, and in one case I have actually been warned not to talk about this with you. But listen to what I say and judge for yourself. As a pastor, as a preacher, as a child of the King, I must preach the Word without fear of the criticism of men. I must preach it with the reverential fear of the love of God for the souls of all men.

"This morning we will deal with a topic that may be uncomfortable to many of you. Some of you will probably be outraged at me. To others it may tell you something you already suspected. To still others it will confirm what you already knew. At the very start I need to assure you that my object is not to attack or challenge any individual man, woman, or child. I sincerely love every one of you here today. What I share with you affects the lives of many men, women, and children. Today I want to talk to you about the subject of Freemasonry and its incompatibility with Christianity."

A murmur shuddered through the congregation, and Jeff waited until it subsided before continuing. He avoided looking directly at his in-laws but could see that Roy had leaned back over the pew and was saying something to Charlie Miller.

"A few weeks ago I was in the Masonic Lodge across the street. I was there because I had petitioned for membership. I stood outside the doors to the inner Lodge room where the Lodge was in session. I was waiting to be inducted into membership. Many members of our church were there as Masons. I had been given the assurance of several members of the Lodge, men for whom I had the highest regard, that I would not be asked to say or do anything that would be contrary to my Christian faith, so I felt reasonably comfortable.

"I went to the Masonic Lodge that night dressed like I'm dressed today, in a business suit. While I waited to be called in, there were several men who were attending to me. Two of them are present here today as members of this church. I do not want to go into all the details of what transpired at that time except to say that they had me remove my suit coat, my shoes and socks, and my tie. I was then told to take off my trousers and slip my left arm out of my shirt so that my arm and breast were bare. They gave me a pair of baggy pants to wear that had one leg cut off at the knee and then blindfolded me and put a noose around my neck." The sanctuary was stirring restlessly as Jeff related the details of the ordeal.

"I guess that while I was expecting it to be a bit 'fraternity' in nature, I hadn't prepared myself to be in such a state. I became quite upset when they required that I remove my wedding ring from my finger. You know, I wanted to stop it all right then, because that ring was the symbol of my love and my fidelity to my wife, Jennifer. But I let it go rather than make a scene, and I allowed myself to fall one step deeper into deception.

"Then there was a knock on the door, the person asked who was there, and the man with me said that I was a poor, blind candidate who had long been in darkness and was seeking the light of that worshipful Lodge. Right there your pastor should have been honest enough to stop the ritual and leave.

"You see, I was *not* a poor blind man in darkness, seeking the light of some secret fraternity. I already was a child of the light, a better light! That light is the light of the Lord and Savior Jesus Christ. In His Word He declared, '*I am the light of the world; he that followeth me shall not walk in darkness, but shall have the light of life.*' I walked into the literal darkness of Masonry that night with a blindfold on, led around a darkened Lodge room while all sorts of men carried on with heavy-sounding, repetitious words of all sorts. I'll spare you the details. Suffice it to say that I left the light of Christ and went into darkness. Today I am ending that darkness and following the one true light, that of God, His Son, and the Holy Spirit. I am hereby officially resigning from Freemasonry from this pulpit. I do so because the Holy Scriptures *demand* that I do!

"The Scriptures call upon us to be children of the light. Open up your Scriptures with me to Ephesians 5, verses 6 to 14, and read with me." Jeff paused until the rustling of a hundred Bibles ceased. When the church was ready to read he continued: " *'Let no man deceive you with vain words, for because of these things cometh the wrath of God upon the children of disobedience. Be not ye therefore partakers with them. For ye were sometimes darkness, but now are ye light in the Lord; walk as children of light (for the fruit of the Spirit is in all goodness and righteousness and truth), proving what is acceptable unto the Lord. And have no fellowship with the unfruitful works of darkness, but rather reprove them. For it is a shame even to speak of those things which are done of them in secret. But all things that are reproved are made manifest by the light, for whatsoever doth make manifest is light. Wherefore he saith, Awake, thou that sleepest, and arise from the dead, and Christ shall give thee light.'*

"Well, I realized that if the Scriptures were true, then when I allowed myself to be blindfolded and seek the light of Masonry, I had stepped out of the light of Christ into the darkness of the Lodge and had actually separated myself from Christ. The Word says that if I were in the dark, I was to rise from the dead as though I were asleep! I was dead to Christ in such a state.

"Dear church, you know what they were saying about your pastor? A born-again Christian pastor? As I came through that Lodge door they said that I was spiritually blind, and they say that about every single Christian coming through the door of that Lodge.

"They weren't talking about the blindfold; that's just the facade. The Masons sit there on the sidelines as the new members come in and the blindfold is on; they assume it's just physical blindness, but the ritual and the words themselves are talking about spiritual blindness.

"I was led into the Lodge room by men sitting here this morning, and they can testify to the truth of this. You go in blindfolded, with cabletow or noose around your neck, and your heart may even be beating a little more rapidly as you hear someone say that he's about to apply a sharp instrument to your naked breast. You stand there waiting to get shot with a needle or feel a knife, but in a split second you feel the point of a compass, the kind you make circles with, and then they lead you on and you're scared because it's all so secretive and you're blindfolded!

"You go through the ritual, and when it's over, about all you can remember is that you've lived through it. And then you're told to kneel for the benefit of prayer, and they say a godless prayer, and then they ask you in whom you put your trust.

"You sure don't put your trust in any of your congregation there who are Masons and who you know are in that place. You'd like to run out but you don't know where the door is because they've moved you around a couple of times and you're blindfolded. And you tell them the only thing you can: that your trust is in God. They say that your trust in God is well-founded. Rise, follow your conductor, and fear no danger, someone says. Whew!

That felt good! You know what that was? That was the lamb being led to the slaughter!

"So I followed along, feeling a lot more comfortable, and was escorted to the altar and told to kneel. I was told just how to place my hand on the Bible, God's Holy Word. I was then required to swear a binding oath or obligation to the fraternity."

Jeff paused for a long quiet moment as he collected his thoughts. This part is really going to be the hardest, he thought to himself. "This oath was administered to me by my father-in-law, Roy Wallace." There was an audible gasp from the congregation as Roy's name was mentioned. "He assured me that the oath would not interfere with my duty to God, myself, and my family. I believed him and I am sad to say I was deceived.

"Part of that oath was that I would promise and swear *without reservation* that I would not reveal the secrets of the Lodge under the penalty of having my throat cut across and my tongue torn out and buried in the sand of the sea. Only then was I able to have the blindfold removed and receive the 'light of the Lodge.'

"Now let me tell you that Jesus Christ is my Lord and I'm *not* bound by any oath that is in violation of His Word. I publicly repent of that oath and renounce it in the name of Jesus Christ! It was He who said in Matthew 5:34-37, *'I say unto you, Swear not at all, neither by heaven, for it is God's throne, nor by the earth, for it is his footstool, neither by Jerusalem, for it is the city of the great King. Neither shalt thou swear by thy head, because thou canst not make one hair white or black. But let your communication be Yea, yea; Nay, nay, for whatsoever is more than these cometh of evil.'* Could it be any clearer to you, church?" he asked.

Jeff continued as the church stirred noisily. "As part of the binding obligations that I swore in the Lodge that night, I bound myself to the members of the Masonic fraternity both here in Badger Lake and throughout the world, I guess. Remember now that Jesus was nowhere lifted up in the entire ritual, because Freemasonry is universal in its declaration of only a belief in God, *any god*. What I did in my spiritual blindness was again strictly forbidden by the Word of God. Read with me 2 Corinthians 6:14-17: *'Be ye not unequally yoked together with unbelievers, for what fellowship hath righteousness with unrighteousness? And what communion hath light with darkness? And what concord hath Christ with Belial? Or what part hath he that believeth with an infidel? And what agreement hath the temple of God with idols? For ye are the temple of the living God; as God hath said, I will dwell in them and walk in them, and I will be their God and they shall be my people. Wherefore come out from among them and be ye separate, saith the Lord, and touch not the unclean thing, and I will receive you.'*

"Church, I sinned deeply when I brought the presence of God within me to that altar and swore an oath that our Lord Jesus Himself declared has come from the evil one!

"Even worse, because of this yoking by blood oath to unbelievers and accepting the false doctrine that God is manifest in any and all deities, when a Mason enters into a Christian house of worship he brings Baal worship into the house of the Lord. Unless I repent of my own participation in such a thing, I would do that every time I step into church and this pulpit. *I repent for this horrid sin before God and this congregation!*"

"Preacher, you better shut your filthy mouth before someone shuts it for you!" screamed someone from the rear of the church. Jeff immediately recognized the voice as that of Stan Fields. The congregation was in an uproar as others shouted back at Fields, who ran from the building, shouting curses back over his shoulder. Mick Sterling rose from his seat and hurriedly followed after him.

"Please, I beg you to be seated!" Jeff cried out again and again. "Please let me finish!" The people finally settled down, more to see what would happen next than for any other reason.

Jeff gripped the sides of the pulpit for support and ground on with his message. "I think the final cap to the deception came at what was called the Apron Lecture. I was told that this lambskin apron was to be my *covering* when I stood naked and alone before that Great White Throne Judgment seat of God. The Bible mentions only one Great White Throne Judgment, and that is found in Revelation chapter 20. That is the judgment place of those who are damned!" Again, the congregation literally shuddered, gasping as in one breath.

"Enough!" screamed Roy Wallace. "Not one word more!"

The entire congregation froze as they watched Roy Wallace lift himself laboriously up from his seat. Roy stared slowly around the sanctuary. "I will not sit here a second longer and listen to one more lying slur against so great a fraternity as Freemasonry, nor should any other Mason present!" Without another word he began making his way out the aisle. Ruth rose and hurried behind him, the pain of the conflict deeply etched on her face.

Charlie Miller stood, ordering his wife to leave with him. "If I hadn't been here this morning, I would never have believed this," he proclaimed to the church at large. They angrily worked their way through the people seated in the row and strode down the aisle.

Men and their wives began rising throughout the congregation. Steve Hanson stood in the center of the aisle, staring in stony silence at Jeff for a full minute before he spun on his heels and sped from the church, his wife hurrying behind him.

When it finally ended, almost half the people had walked out of the church, leaving the remnant of the congregation in stunned silence.

"Mark this day," Jeff spoke softly, "because it is one in which you and the rest of this congregation must choose whether you will serve the Lord in His sanctuary or the Lords of the Lodge." Jeff stepped around the pulpit and came down into the aisle. "I thank God that you have remained here, and I ask you to pray for the church, for those brothers and sisters who have left and for Jenny and me. Please," he cried out, "come forward to the altar area and let's join in prayer before we leave this place today."

Jenny worked her way through the crowd filling the altar area and placed her arm around Jeff's waist. Her face was wet with tears. "I know you're right, Jeff, I know you are!" she cried. "But how can I stand so hard against my own mother and father? Dear God, I wish we had never come here!" she sobbed as he turned and held her tightly to him.

Win and Sue Johnson were at their side and put their arms around the couple. "Trust the Lord in this, Jenny," Sue said gently. "Jeff was right and we needed to face this thing as a whole congregation. Jeff did the right thing, and your mom and dad will come to understand it. Trust in God, Jenny."

Jeff could see Betty and Mick in the back, praying with a group by the door. He was surprised to see that Tom Adams, who had left with the Masons, had stepped back into the church and was standing to the side, watching in grim silence.

The afternoon was a blur of phone calls and visits as members of the church called or stopped in to talk to Jeff and Jenny. The Sterlings and the Johnsons spent most of their afternoon at the parsonage, running interference on the phone and at the door. Jeff was grateful for the support and encouragement, but he could see that his wife was in a state of despair over her parents' reaction to Jeff's words. An intense visit from a number of her Job's Daughters group left her weeping in the kitchen as Sue and Betty spoke to her in quiet tones.

Betty Sterling had finally insisted that Jeff and Jennifer spend a little time resting alone during the late afternoon. "Listen, loves! You two are an absolute mess and you need to talk sweet to each other and catch a few winks before you end up in the frying pan again." They wisely and gratefully obeyed her stern directive.

"Jeff, you're my husband and I truly trust you," Jennifer whispered as she lay there on the bed at his side. "If you feel that our involvement in Masonry causes us in any way to be weakened in our walk with Christ, then we have to step away from it." The tears welled up in her eyes as she continued. "But it hurts so much to have it make my mom and dad so angry." The tears turned to weeping and Jenny choked out great sobs of pain that shook the bed.

Jeff held her for a long time. "Will you please forgive me, Jen?" he asked, his eyes moistening over as he fought his own tears. "This whole thing is my own fault. If I had never agreed to join the Lodge, if I had never agreed to let you work with the Jobies, we could have maybe somehow avoided all this."

"That's not true, Jeff," she answered. Jenny rolled over and sat up next to him, rubbing the tears from her eyes before resting her elbows on his chest. "You said this morning that bringing Freemasonry into the church is the same as bringing Baal worship into the congregation. If that's really true, and you knew it, you were going to have to stand up to it sooner or later."

"I guess I wasn't as ready for that 'sooner' as I might have thought," Jeff laughed gently. As he watched her return his laughter, he knew their own crisis was over. "It's one of those 'Trust in the Lord in all ways' times, Jen. Let's go into church tonight as a team, okay?"

The evening service held a few surprises for Jeff. He was used to seeing a reasonably small crowd on Sunday night, but this evening the pews were packed and the undercurrent of normally light conversation was tense and animated. Several of the Masons who had left during the morning service were back, most notably Steve Hanson and Tom Adams.

As he scanned the audience from the platform during the opening music, Jeff was astonished to see Tiny sitting in the far corner of the back pew. When Jeff had approached him during the summer about coming to church, Tiny had made it graphically clear that he would come to church for the first time when the underworld had frozen over. Apparently that day had come to Badger Lake.

Jeff's eyes locked on those of his wife. She smiled a tiny smile of encouragement. She had made her way through the tough times of the afternoon and was in control of her emotions now.

Jeff walked up to the pulpit and the conversations came to an immediate halt. "I came to church tonight more to be with the saints of the Lord than to preach another sermon like this morning," he said. "There is a tape of the morning service that will be available as soon as I can get it duplicated this week, and for those of you who were not there, it would be easiest for you to get a copy for your own study rather than hear it all second- and third-hand. Meanwhile let me say just a few things about it and then we can get on with lifting Jesus up instead of laboring over this conflict.

"Someone gave me a book about Freemasonry this afternoon and I scanned through some of the pages before I came over tonight. I was happy to discover that I'm not the first to stand up and to speak out against it. I'm just, perhaps, the latest."

Jeff opened a book he held in his hand and continued. "I'm going to share with you the names of a remarkable list of great Christian men and statesmen who renounced the Lodges and opposed them, and this is particularly important to you if you happen to be upset and just waiting to take a piece out of my hide, because one of the most illustrious figures in religion to speak out against Masonry was a man by the name of John Wesley. Yes, I'm talking about one of the greatest religious reformers in the history of the modern world— right back to the very root of Methodism. That was the man who left his church and preached the salvation message to miners throughout England. Yes, John Wesley took a stand against Masonry. So did great men like Alexander Campbell, Daniel Webster, Wendell Phillips, Chief Justice Charles Marshall, Charles Sumner, John Hancock, Horace Greeley, Dwight L. Moody, R. A. Torrey, Timothy Dwight, Charles Finney, Charles Blanchard, John Adams, John Quincy Adams, John Madison, Amos Wells, Simon Peter Long, and James M. Gray.

"Listen to the words of Dwight L. Moody that he directed to a group of pastors. I only wish I had read them a few days before I joined the Lodge. Let me read them to you. *'I don't see how any Christian, most of all a Christian minister, can go into these secret lodges with unbelievers. They say they have more influence for good but I say they can have more influence for good by staying out of them and then reproving their evil deeds. Abraham was more influence for good in Sodom than Lot was for good. True reformers separate themselves from the world rather than becoming a part of it. But, Dwight L. Moody, some say, if you talk that way you'll drive all the members of secret societies out of your meetings and out of your churches. What if I did? Better men will take their places. Give them the truth anyway, and if they would rather leave their churches than their Lodges, the sooner they get out of the churches, the better. I would rather have ten members who are separated from the world than a thousand such members. Come out of your lodges. Better one with God than a thousand without Him.'*

"Close to half our church is involved in the Lodge, and most of them walked out of this church today. There is no victory in that, and we must pray tonight that the Lord will open their blind eyes and restore these brothers and sisters and their families to us. But we must be prepared to accept the fact that this church has been ripped apart. Many will say that I have caused it to happen, when in fact the Word of God has required it. I pray that every Mason and Eastern Star will flee from the altar of Baal and come back into fellowship before the altar of the living God.

"Now before I get away from the just and true cause for our being in this place tonight, let me say simply that I do not have the strength to give you a sermon tonight. Psalm 134 is very short, but appropriate for a time like tonight. It says, *'Behold, bless ye the Lord, all ye servants of the Lord, which by night stand in the house of the Lord. Lift up your hands in the sanctuary, and bless the Lord. The Lord that made heaven and earth bless thee out of Zion.'*

179

"I would just like to ask the choir and the music team—what's left of you, anyway—to come up and lead us in a time of worship. Let's praise the Lord, those of us who stand here in the house of the Lord tonight. I'm going to go down and sit with my wife for awhile!

——————◆——————

The lights burned long into the night at the Lodge that Sunday night. There had been a large number of cars in front of the Lodge when Jeff and Jenny walked over to the church for the evening service, and they were still there when they finally went to bed. Jeff could only imagine what was taking place, but it was well past midnight when he heard the cars start up and leave.

The phone woke him early in the morning. It was Win Johnson who called to tell him that Roy Wallace had called a special church board meeting for that night, to be held at the church. Roy wanted him to pass on the information to Jeff with the instruction that the pastor was *not* to be in attendance by authority of a remote clause in the church constitution that allowed for such a meeting without the pastor, in the event that disciplinary action against the pastor was to be discussed.

"Don't get too upset, Jeff," Win concluded. "I'm still a board member, and no one is going to hold any kangaroo court while I'm there. By the way, Jeff, Mick gave me some material last night that he sent away for to a ministry near Seattle. One of the items is a little book called '*The Question of Freemasonry.*' It has quite a compact presentation of the Christian view on Freemasonry. I'll bring it over sometime today, unless you can stop by the store and pick it up. It should encourage you."

Jeff dragged himself out of bed, groaning under the sheer weight of the pressures he felt. Jennifer was still in a deep sleep, exhausted both physically and emotionally from the events of the previous day. She hadn't even stirred when the phone rang. He struggled over the simple effort to put on his sweats and socks and lace up his jogging shoes.

I may die this morning and just lie there in the middle of the street until someone finds me, he thought as he descended the stairs. I can't believe I ache so much this morning. I need to jog a few extra miles today and shake some of these cobwebs out. Moses was carrying on at the front door like he was going to tear right through it if Jeff didn't open it up for him pretty soon. He had been Jeff's jogging partner for several months now, and aggressively awaited each morning's run with the abandon of a fanatic.

It was an unusually cold and rainy day, but Jeff warmed quickly and reached his face to the rain, enjoying the feeling of it hitting against him. He jogged west toward the lake until he came to the perimeter of the town and the bridge across the Beaverhead River. He turned north and ran along the east bank, stopping only for a few moments to laugh as Moses leaped into the shallows to chase a duck and her brood in a hopeless contest of skill and speed. With the mother duck scolding him loudly,

Moses happily splashed his way back to Jeff, shaking a major portion of the river over him in a joyous reunion.

Jeff finally reached another bridge and a gravel access road several miles north of the town and jogged the short mile or so back to the four-lane. As he turned south toward Badger Lake again, a blue pickup truck with two men in it approached him heading north. He recognized the driver as Stan Fields and waved a hello, but Stan stared straight ahead and sped past him. Jeff caught a glimpse of the passenger, the man he only knew as Duane, one of the men from his initiation to the Lodge. That is going to be a difficult fence to rebuild, he thought as he picked up his pace and continued on.

By the time he reached the Grange, Jeff was as thoroughly drenched as if he had chased ducks with Moses. Glancing back, he noticed that the blue pickup was keeping pace with him, several hundred yards back. I suppose they're playing a little game of intimidation, he thought. I hope they're ready for a long wait if they think they're going to frighten me. Yet, as he jogged into town, Jeff could feel the presence of the men behind him, and the feeling made the hair on the back of his neck tingle. He didn't like it.

Win's van was already at the store as Jeff passed up Tiny's and went directly across the lot and entered the back door of the hardware store. The pickup stopped at the edge of the lot and waited.

"Win," Jeff shouted. "Mr. Popularity is here."

Win Johnson laughed as he walked back to greet his friend. "Well, you sure are popular in the Johnson household, old buddy! Remember, even if half the town is ready to lynch you, the other half will love you to death."

"Either way, I'm a goner!" Jeff replied with a gaiety that he forced into his voice. He was shocked that he was shaking, as much from the encounter with the pickup as he was with being wet from head to foot. "I *really* need some coffee and something to dry myself off with," he said as he noticed Win's concern over his condition.

As he sat there by the front counter with an old towel over his shoulders and some hot coffee working its way into his bones, he felt like a new man. The blue pickup was now parked across the street from the front door of the hardware store. "Win, Stan Fields and his buddy, Duane somebody-or-other, have been following me in Stan's pickup. I think it's their idea of neighborly harassment. I'm not too sure how to handle it."

Win walked to the door and took a long look at the truck. "I'll have a little word with our friend, Stan. He didn't have too good a day yesterday. That's Duane Thorpe with him. Duane is our local Neanderthal man. He's on some kind of government disability and works as a caretaker on one of the ranches east of town. Strange guy.

"Look, Jeff, things aren't going to be a bed of roses around here for a little while, so get tough! You have some mighty good people who will be right at your side every minute until this thing is worked out." Win smiled at his drenched friend. "Tonight the good old boys are going to chew on your good name for awhile and get it out of their

183

system. Then it's going to be the long slow road to recovery. Sue and I have probably had six calls from other families who had left the church over this issue and they are excited about coming back. Everything is going to work out for the good!" he assured Jeff as he gave him one of those loving claps on the back that would drive a steer to its knees.

"Boy, I don't want to be around you when you get really happy," Jeff laughed as he juggled his spilling coffee cup.

———————◆———————

Win climbed the stairs of the Education Building to the second floor and walked into the conference room where the board meetings were held. Roy Wallace, Charlie Miller, Steve Hanson, and Walter Tate were already seated. Walter was the only surprise. He was elderly and frail and rarely made it to church during bad weather. They had been meaning to replace him on the board for some time now, but like so many other things, it kept being put off till later.

"Thank you for coming, Win," Roy Wallace said. "This will be a very brief meeting, since we have only one item."

This was not going to be a friendly meeting, Win reflected.

"The entire board is here, with the exception of Jeff Moore," Roy continued coldly. "I have called this meeting in accordance with our bylaws so that we might review disciplinary action against the pastor. As Chairman, I therefore call the meeting to order. Charlie Miller, Board Secretary, will tape-record the meeting for the record." Again, Win was struck by the total lack of emotion on the faces around the table.

Roy Wallace gave his rough interpretation of the events that led up to and encompassed Jeff's ministry the day before. No one else spoke as he related what he presented as the most outrageous, offensive act that a man of the cloth could ever bring upon a congregation.

"This is the most despicable thing I have ever witnessed in all my Christian life," he concluded. "I therefore bring a motion before the board that Jeff Moore be fired as the Pastor of Badger Lake Baptist Church, effective immediately. He will remove his personal effects from the church within 24 hours and not return to the building. He must be out of the parsonage within 30 days. He will be paid severance of 90 days pay when he surrenders the keys to the church building tomorrow."

Roy paused and turned to look at the other men. "That's to help him get on the road and out of here. He certainly deserves to be put onto the street without a penny."

"Roy, for heaven's sake!" Win cried out. "This is your son-in-law and daughter you are talking about. Stop this insanity!"

"I second the motion," interjected Charlie Miller. "Please call the vote." Steve Hanson sat frozen in place, his eyes straight ahead. Walter Tate looked about the room, seemingly oblivious to what was taking place.

"The motion has been made and seconded," Roy said. "Let's vote the motion."

"Now wait a minute, all of you," Win interrupted. "I demand that we discuss the question before us. Over 50 percent of this church was in agreement with the actions of our pastor, and you are trying to railroad this young man of God solely because he opened up your little secret fraternity to the light of the Word of God. I demand that you stop this evil work and repent before God."

"You can demand anything you want, Johnson," Charlie Miller snapped, "but if you don't shut up and vote the motion, you had better move out of town along with your filthy little liar of a minister."

Roy Wallace pushed on, his voice raised in anger. "The motion has been called for a vote. All in favor say aye!" The four men responded in unison.

"All opposed say nay!"

"Why bother to give you that satisfaction?" Win said darkly. "You are pathetic excuses for real men. It makes me sick to just look at your smirking faces." He turned and stared in unbelief at Roy Wallace. "How can any father do what you are doing to your only child? Are your oaths of obedience to the Lodge above even your love for her? Don't you see that you are going to live to dearly regret this night?" he pleaded.

"Please note that Win Johnson voted the single negative vote," Roy continued. "The motion is carried by a vote of 4 to 1. Charlie, please type a letter of dismissal and deliver it tonight to the former pastor and his little wife."

He rose from his seat and faced Win. "You're the one who is going to wish this night never took place, Johnson. You are the one who just cut his own throat! This meeting is adjourned." He spun and walked briskly toward the door. The other men followed silently.

"Roy!" Win shouted after him. "Tell Stan Fields to leave those kids alone or he will have me to deal with, real quick!"

Win left the building and went directly to the parsonage, where Jennifer and Jeff greeted him anxiously. "I've never been more upset in my life. In a few minutes, Charlie Miller will be delivering a letter notifying you that you have been fired, Jeff. They had the whole thing planned before the meeting ever took place."

"Frankly, Win, we expected it. There was no way the Lodge would allow me to continue to pastor after embarrassing them the way I did. Yet for the life of me, I don't know how I could have done anything other than what I did," Jeff answered. "We are at peace about it."

Win looked over at Jenny and knew that things were under control. "I'm so sorry, Jenny. I know your dad will come around eventually."

"I called my mom while dad was at the meeting," Jennifer told him. She smiled wistfully. "She hung up on me."

"You know your mom loves you, Jen," Jeff said, responding to the obvious pain in her eyes. "We have to pray for her. What a terrible situation for her to be in!"

Moments later, Charlie Miller knocked at the door and silently shoved an envelope into Jeff's outstretched hand. He glared at Win for a second and disappeared into the night. Jeff noticed the blue pickup sitting across the street and waved at the dark figures sitting in it.

"Let's get a good night's sleep," Win suggested, "and get together with the Sterlings and a few of the other church folks tomorrow and work through this thing. It's far from over!"

───────◆───────

Both Jeff and Jennifer bolted upright as though the house had been struck by lightning. The fire siren, on top of the fire station just 150 yards away, pierced through their very beings as it screamed its warning to the entire community. Jeff threw his sweats and shoes on and raced out of the house, Jenny a split second behind him. Jeff could see the reflection of the flames from the upstairs window as he reached the stairs. Something was burning brightly on the main business street, a block away.

"O dear Lord!" Jennifer cried out. "It's the hardware store! It's Win's store!" They ran to the edge of the sidewalk, raising their hands against the heat as the volunteer firemen began spraying water against the building.

Win Johnson came bursting past them, running into the store. "I've got to get my records!" he cried as he disappeared inside, pushing his screaming wife toward them as he went.

Jeff stood riveted to the spot, frozen in shocked horror as he watched Win race into the flaming interior. "Win!" he screamed over the roar of the fire, "Get out of there! Get out of there!" He could see Win trying to drag a file cabinet bare-handed from behind the counter. His shirt was on fire. The flames were all around him as he tripped and went to his knees.

Jeff let out an animal groan, and with Sue and Jennifer shrieking in his ears he leaped into the building. Fighting his way through the smoke and flames to his fallen friend, he grabbed Win under the arms and dragged him to the door, where the firemen yanked him away, desperately fighting the flames that covered his upper body. Jeff could hear the wailing cry of Sue as she fought to reach her husband. Other men dragged Jeff out onto the street and sprayed water on his smoldering clothes. He could smell the stench of his own burning hair as Jenny held him tightly in her arms, sobbing in her relief that he was safe.

The medics and Sue were already loading Win into the ambulance to race him to the hospital in Dillon, and the two could only cling to each other and stare in disbelief as they watched the entire building fill with flames. Jeff could see the file cabinet totally consumed by the flames. His eye caught a glimpse of Jennifer's picture among the hundreds of photos as it curled up into the flaming wall. As the ambulance pulled away, its siren screaming above the din, Jeff knelt with his wife in the middle of the chaos. "Dear Lord," he prayed, "please save

Win. Save him from the devourer. Put Your protecting hands upon his body and save him, O Lord!"

They stood up, almost falling again under the embrace of Mick and Betty as they rushed upon the scene. "Dear Father in heaven, is everyone all right?" Mick shouted. "What a horrible sight!" He stepped back from them and cried out, "Jeff, your hair is all but burned off! What happened here, lad?"

When Jeff told them of the horror of almost losing Win and that the ambulance was now racing for the Dillon hospital, Betty grabbed Mick by the arm and tugged him toward the cars down the street. "Come on, love! We need to be there for Sue when they get there!"

"This place is gone, Jeff," Mick said quickly, looking at the collapsing building. "You get home and get some salve on those burns or get to the hospital, where you can get some medicine on you. Go along now!" he ordered.

Jeff looked back at the old wooden building. It was already gutted, and the main effort of the firefighters was now to protect the nearby buildings from going up in flames with it. Jenny clung tightly to him as they hurried back toward home.

As they turned the corner and headed toward the church property, Jenny cried out, "Jeff, there goes that awful Stan Fields and his buddy running out from behind the church!" Jeff looked up to see the two men dart from around the Education Building and run down the street. One was Stan Fields, the other Duane Thorpe.

"Let them run, Jenny! I'll bet they know something about how that fire got started. I'll talk to the police about them tomorrow. Let's get the car and get to the hospital."

As they ran up the stairs of the porch, Jennifer collapsed to the floor screaming. Jeff could see that she fell onto something covered with blood. As he knelt beside her, he realized it was Moses.

"O No! No! No! No!" she cried. "They killed my puppy, my puppy. Jeff, they killed my puppy!"

It took all of Jeff's strength to pull his wife away from the body of the dog. He felt for a pulse and found it still there, feeble but still there. "Jenny, there's a pulse!" he shouted. "He's still alive!" Jeff could see that the dog had been shot through the shoulder, into the chest area. The bleeding needed to be slowed down or they would never get him to the vet. "Jenny! Push your fingers right here to slow down the blood. Stay with him so I can call the vet and get the car!"

Moments later they were praying aloud for God to spare their pet as they raced toward Dillon, the puppy and Jenny covered with blood. "Jeff," she cried out through her tears, "what kind of animals would do a thing like this? Do you think my own father let them do this?"

"I can't imagine that your father would let them shoot your dog, Jenny, no matter how angry he was. I just can't imagine it."

The vet and an assistant were waiting as they drove up, and within seconds they had Moses on a table, hooking up equipment to him. The vet was working an IV into the dog and yelled at them to get out of his way and leave the operating room. Jeff took Jennifer gently by the arm and guided her into the waiting room. "It's going to be okay, honey! It's going to be okay! We got him here alive and he's going to pull out of it. You'll see!" He wasn't sure if he was trying to console his wife or himself at the moment.

Jeff called over to the hospital and notified their shocked friends of the latest events. Win was stabilized but had some pretty bad burns. Sue wept as she shared the news.

Hours passed as the vet worked to save the dog. Jeff and Jennifer slept and paced and prayed as the time dragged on. Mick and Betty came over after they were assured that Win would sleep through the rest of the night. Betty put her arms around Jennifer and comforted the distressed young woman. "It's going to be okay, Jenny. Just trust the Lord to fix things up! Even Sue is asleep right now, on a cot in the room right by Win's bed."

Jeff shared what had happened at the board meeting with them as they both shook their heads in dismay.

"A dirty bit of business for the Lodge this night, loves!" Mick said. "I've seen it like this in England and Scotland, but never been in the middle of it like this before." He looked at the burned and seared young man and shook his head. "Jeff, you're a warrior prince of a man! We'll rout these maniacs to the very last man. Either set them free or send them scurrying! We're not going to give up our church and our pastor without a bigger fight than they're ready for! Amen?"

CHAPTER EIGHT

"Amen, Mick, Amen," Jeff responded.

They all turned as the vet came into the room. "Well," he smiled, "we have one very badly damaged young dog in there, but with a lot of rest and TLC he's going to pull through. It's a miracle that he made it. A few more minutes in getting him here and he would have been gone. He's a very lucky little puppy."

The dam of tears broke loose from the deepest reservoir within Jenny and she wept openly with relief. Too many things had happened in one day for her to hold back any longer. "Can we go in and see him?" she asked through the sobs.

"You bet you can," the vet answered. "But just remember, he isn't going to be awake and aware of what's happening around him for a day or two. It's going to be several weeks before I would even think about letting him go home."

"That's okay," Jeff responded. "It's just enough to see him still alive and breathing." He and Jenny followed the vet into the operating room while the Sterlings sat there smiling at each other.

"I think it's time to get busy setting some things in order, Mick. What do you think, love?" Betty asked.

Chapter
9

It was only a few hours later, early the next morning, when Jeff quietly left his still-sleeping wife and made his way back to the hardware store. Tiny had yet to arrive to open the cafe for the day, and the morning had a crispness to it that carried the smell of the still-smoldering fire throughout the whole business district. The store had been reduced to rubble; there was literally nothing left.

"Lord," Jeff prayed quietly, "You said in Your Word that all things work to the good for those who love You and are called according to Your purpose. Where's the good here, today, Lord?"

Tears were welling up in Jeff's eyes as he relived the terrible events of the night before. He stood at the place that was once the entrance to the store. "Show it to me so I can proclaim it to Your glory. I just have a hard time seeing it through all this destruction." Jeff's eyes fell on the remains of the file cabinet that Win was so bent on saving. It had almost cost him his life.

He turned to see Tiny walking over from the cafe. "Hard to believe, isn't it?" Tiny commented gruffly as he came to Jeff's side. "That old building has been here longer than I can remember. Used to be the place where everyone stopped in to get the news before the cafe was built. Old man Johnson had an old hound named Blue who laid out in that doorway. You had to step over him to get in the store. The old man was a Mason. He played the game like everyone else around here. Heard you were the hero here last night. How is Win doing, Jeff?"

Jeff filled him in on the events at the fire, the hospital, and the vet, sharing his deep concern for Win Johnson and his family. Tiny listened intently, shaking his head in obvious revulsion over the details. "Win Johnson wouldn't go along with them. Never would. They kind of let it go, mostly because of his dad, until he told them to get their hands off you. They're a lovable bunch of folks around here, but sure set in their ways!"

Tiny laughed. "I'll tell you what, Jeff. I heard a TV preacher talk about the apostle Paul one time. He said that wherever Paul went, there was either revival or riots, and sometimes both! Boy, he sure was talking about you that day!"

Jeff grinned back for a moment, then his face became dark. "Tiny, where do you fit in all this? You're not a Mason, yet they all practically live at your cafe. How have you managed to walk in among all this and yet stay apart from it all?"

"Well, the answer is easier than you might think. I just don't fit in at all. My grandfolks came up from Salt Lake City with the railroad. My granddad was a wild-eyed old Mormon preacher with two wives, and they really came up here so they could live what we called *The Principle*, or polygamy. I grew up with two mamas! They were cooking for the crews then, and I'm still here cooking for them now. I'm just an old Jack Mormon who knows better than to sign up with the Masons. Lot of bad blood between the Mormons and the Masons, and I'm a lot more scared of old Brigham and his destroying angels waiting up there for me in spirit prison than I am of any bunch of Masons.

"Anyway," he sighed, "both my grandfather and my father made it awfully plain to the Masons around here that they were all bound for hell for killing old Joe Smith. These guys may sure think I'm a great cook, but the old feuds don't go away so easy. The Masons got it figured that the Mormons stole their lodge rituals and secrets and stuck them in the Mormon temple ceremonies. Joseph Smith supposedly said that God told him to do it. Some figure that's why they killed him. They don't own enough blackballs over there in the lodge to hold a vote on this old Mormon being a Mason."

Tiny paused for a moment, looking up into Jeff's face intently. "I never met a preacher in my whole life I thought much of, *including* the Mormons and the Baptists. You're the first one who I ever saw take it on the chin squarely for what the Good Book says. You've got grit, Jeff. Don't let them bully you out of town. You have the power to put an end to this good-old-boy system and make this tragedy here last night count for something. They may have done an evil thing here, but I'll bet my money that if you set your jaw in this, *something really good* is how it's going to end up." Tiny smiled and turned back toward the cafe.

Jeff watched the heavy man walk across the lot to the cafe and smiled. He felt a tremendous weight lift off him and knew that talking with Tiny this morning was no accident. "Thank You, Lord," he prayed. "Thank You for sending Tiny here with Your word for me this morning. I *do* trust in You and I can't wait to see what You have set in motion!" He turned from the ruin and ran with an easy gait toward home.

Jennifer was still asleep when he returned. He sat on the front steps, shaking his head from time to time as he thought over the things Tiny had told him. Jeff could still hardly believe that Tiny was a Mormon all this time and he never knew it. His eyes fell on the bloodstains where they had found Moses, and his face turned hard as he thought of the two men they saw running away last night. We have some accounts to settle, he thought as he rose. First, I've got to get this deck cleaned up before Jenny wakes up.

———————◆———————

They were just finishing breakfast when Mick and Betty burst in the door. "Jeff!" Mick shouted, "I've got some great news! Your dear old chum spent the wee hours digging through a copy of the church's

Articles of Incorporation and Bylaws. It seems that what was good for their goose is good for our gander."

Pointing to the coffee cup in Jeff's hand, he grimaced a bit and then smiled. "Short of deeply offending the Queen Mother, I'd love a cup of that black stuff you Colonials have substituted for the drink of the Crown."

Coffee in hand, Mick pointed to the papers he had laid out on the table in front of Jeff. "They were in the right when they called their special board meeting last night without you being there. But the very next paragraph in the same section allows for 25 percent of the general membership to call a formal business meeting, without board approval. They can set up a special meeting or use any regular meeting time for that purpose."

The older man beamed across the table at the young pastor. "The general membership of the church has almost doubled this year since you came. All those people you have been calling forward in church as new members now outnumber the Masons who walked out last week. Getting 25 percent of the membership to sign a notice for a special business meeting is going to be a breeze!"

"We have a copy of the church directory and a team of people who are meeting with us at noon," Betty added. "They have been calling since six this morning, asking how to help. No one can believe what happened here last night. Mick typed up a letter and the form for the signatures, and we'll be visiting every single family in the church, the Masons included."

Mick handed Jeff and Jenny each a large envelope. "This is an information package we will be handing out at every single home we go to. It has some Christian material on Freemasonry, including the booklet *The Question of Freemasonry.* That alone should cause every real Christian in that crowd to flee it as though the demons of hell were after him."

He pulled a white sheet from Jeff's envelope. "This is a letter explaining how they have taken an unrighteous control of our church and fired you for speaking out. We're calling for a business meeting for this next regular Sunday service time and will vote to dismiss every Mason from the board, restore you as pastor, and add a section to the bylaws prohibiting any member of a secret society from ever holding office in our church again. There is a Christian Proclamation regarding Freemasonry in that envelope which we intend to use as the model for our new section of the bylaws."

"What do you want us to do, Mick?" Jeff asked.

"The best thing you can do is to stay on the sidelines and take care of your little wife and her puppy. I'm driving down to talk to Win about a few things and Sue is already back there with the kids."

Mick rose from his seat at the table. "We have to hurry along. Betty has some helpers coming to finish up the stuffing and I've got to be back in town by 12." The older couple hugged their way out of the house and ran for their car as Jenny and Jeff watched from the door.

Jenny shook her head in awe over the energy of the two older people. "This is going to be some week ahead for us," she said as she wrapped herself into her husband's arms. "You sure are a pretty sight without eyebrows!" she laughed.

————◆————

Sue was sitting at her husband's side when Mick came in the room. Win was lying on his stomach, with something that looked like wet cheesecloth covering the better portion of his entire back. He groaned a weak hello into the pillow. His hands were also covered with the same material and his head was covered with some kind of salve. Win had lost most of the hair from the back of his head in the fire.

"You sure are a pretty sight," Mick said. "Actually, you *really are* a pretty sight. You're alive, and that's the most important thing to your family and your friends. What would we ever have done if we lost you last night?"

Win tried a small smile. "I guess it was a pretty foolish thing. I really thought I was dead. I can't believe Jeff plucked me out of there the way he did. I'm no lightweight." It was obvious that every word out of his mouth was painful.

Sue had tears in her eyes. "I can't stop crying. Every time I look at him, Mick, I cry again. I'm so grateful to God for his life." She pointed to the material covering the burns on his back. "He took the brunt of the flames on his back, his head, and the back of his hands. The doctors say that this new bandage material is like Teflon and will act just like his real skin in a few days."

Mick squeezed her hand. "He's going to be as good as new before we know it, Sue. Just be sure he gets all the ice cream he can eat until he's up and around." They both laughed. Win's reputation for his consumption of ice cream was legendary.

Mick filled them in on the plans for the business meeting and the status of Jennifer and Jeff, answering their questions as he went along.

"The County Police were here already," Sue told him. "They said the fire was arson. Someone had poured gallons of gasoline all through the building. They didn't even try to hide it. They think they know who did it."

"Jeff and Jennifer saw Stan Fields and his pal, Duane Thorpe, running away from their house just before they found their dog shot," Mick responded.

"The police were going to see them at the parsonage when they left here," she informed him. "Maybe those two hoodlums will still be around town, gloating over their revenge with their friends. Poor Jennifer must be beside herself with her dad being so involved. This is such a mess!"

Mick came around past Sue and knelt by the head of the bed, next to Win, and spoke softly to the couple. "Betty and I want you both to know that we love you and can only *imagine* the turmoil you must be going through this morning over the loss of your store. We have a pretty sizable nest egg sitting in the bank and we want to offer it to you to rebuild the store as soon as you can get on your feet."

The Johnsons were stunned by his offer. Win turned his head slowly toward Mick. "I'm overwhelmed, Mick, by your offer, and we just may take you up on a floater loan while we're getting back on our feet, but if there's one thing I can thank Roy Wallace for, its being overinsured." He chuckled softly. "Maybe that's the reason Roy had them torch the old place."

"You don't actually think Roy was behind this, do you?" his wife asked.

"Well, he may not have lit the match, but no Mason in Badger Lake is going to burn down a building insured by Roy Wallace without first getting his okay, I can promise you that."

The Johnson kids burst back into the room, returning from having just emptied a good portion of the hospital cafeteria. Their dad's appetite was apparently hereditary. Mick stood slowly to his feet. "I brought some anointing oil, Win. I'm sure you wouldn't mind if your family and I prayed for you."

———————◆———————

The week sped by in a haze of activity. Stan Fields and Duane Thorpe had been arrested and taken to the County Court in Dillon and charged with the arson fire. They had been released on bail, and were back in town somewhere. It had been years since a felony crime had been committed in Badger Lake, and the local police chief, an elderly man who rarely ventured out of City Hall, wisely called in the County Police. There were too many Masons in Badger Lake for him to attempt to handle the crime, he had told them.

By week's end, over 500 information packages had been personally distributed by the action team put together by Mick and Betty Sterling. Not only had they collected the signatures of 25 percent of the church members, but that number had grown to almost 50 percent by Friday.

People began arriving at the church two hours before the service on Sunday morning. A noisy group gathered in the Education Building around the coffeepot, talking about the fire and the arrests. The pews themselves were filling fast, but the mood inside the church sanctuary was somber. Sue Johnson and her children sat at the center of the front pew, silent and reflective. A few people came up and quietly whispered to her, as though they were at a funeral.

It was obvious that every Mason in the county was there, filling up the seats from the second row back. None seemed to want to be seated anywhere near the Johnsons. Roy Wallace and his wife took their usual seats, as did most of the Masons who were members of the church. With only minutes left to go before the meeting would start, the entire church was filled beyond its capacity. Many members were still outside, unable to gain entry.

Mick Sterling worked his way through the crowded foyer and made his way to the pulpit. A murmur ran through the congregation as many of the Masons began to vocalize their discontent with the proceedings.

Mick tapped the microphone and then began to read from a notepad he held before him. "This business meeting of the membership of Badger Lake Baptist Church is called to order. By the written authority of over 25 percent of the general membership and in accordance with the constitutional bylaws of the corporation, this is a legal meeting of the church for the purpose of conducting the business of the church, and I have been selected to act as chair for the meeting."

Roy Wallace stood. "What evidence do we have that you really do have more than 25 percent of the membership's signatures?" He sat down amid the loud support of the Masonic group around him.

Mick answered quickly. "A panel of six general members has verified each signature and prepared the agenda for this meeting. Would that panel please stand to identify itself and confirm the count." The members of the group stood at their various places and waved their confirmation of the count when asked.

Mick continued. "The first order of business this day is to notify the membership that the church board has fired Pastor Jeff Moore and forbidden him from entering this building. It is the desire of the chair that this order be rescinded and that Pastor Moore and his wife be rightfully seated in this meeting before we proceed further. Do I have a motion?"

Masons throughout the church began to hoot and shout. Sue Johnson stood and quietly responded, "I so move." A voice shouted, "I second that!" Mick leaned into the microphone. "You men are a disgrace to behave this way in a house of worship and show the true nature of your fraternity by your acts. I demand that you be silent." They kept up an undercurrent of complaining until Sue stood again and turned to face them directly. They quieted down and Mick continued.

"All in favor, say aye." He received a loud response. "All opposed, say nay." The Masons again roared their disapproval. Mick stood before them for a long minute, watching as the Masons brought havoc to the meeting.

He signaled to a man standing at the side entry, who immediately turned and headed toward the church offices. Moments later he returned with a half-dozen County Policemen, who stationed themselves across the front of the now-quiet church. Mick returned to the microphone.

"We will not tolerate another outburst from you men. Either be silent or we will have you removed from the building! Now, church members and church members only are permitted to vote. By the raising of your hand, those in favor of the motion please vote now." Hands rose from every direction.

"All opposed?" Again, almost every Mason in the church raised his hand.

"The yes votes carry it," he announced. "My wife, Betty, is in the rear and will bring in the pastor." The church was silent for the short time it took for Jeff and Jennifer to walk to the front and sit by the Johnson family.

"Pastor," Mick called out, "please come and sit in your usual seat up here, at the side of the pulpit. You might like the opportunity to face your accusers in the open." Jeff walked quickly to the stage, whispered something briefly to Mick, and sat looking out at the congregation. His eyes locked on those of his father-in-law.

"The pastor has called something to my attention. This is a formal business meeting of our church. While our bylaws allow for the attendance of nonvoting visitors, they must give up space for voting members who are standing outside, unable to get in the door. Starting with the second row, I must insist that all nonmembers stand and leave the building until all members are seated."

This announcement brought loud cries from the Masons, who had crowded the front of the church. The meeting was in chaos again for 15 minutes while the police physically removed dozens of angry, shouting men.

Just as things settled down again, Charlie Miller stood. "I am a voting member of this congregation and I move that this meeting be adjourned!" Another Masonic member shouted a second. A quick vote dismissed the move, but several others stood and began shouting motions for votes.

"This meeting will be run in an orderly fashion and according to the printed agenda that was distributed in the foyer. If you continue to disrupt the meeting, you will be removed as a disorderly person."

Mick peered at his notes. "The next item is a motion to remove the church board from office, with the obvious exception of Win Johnson. This motion calls for the removal from office of Roy Wallace, Charlie Miller, Steve Hanson, and Walter Tate. The justification for their removal is their underhanded and unchristian use of their office to take revenge against the pastor for his stand on the subject of Freemasonry."

As the crowd of Masons again clamored their anger, Mick waved them down. "I am now going to allow any of the men named in the motion to stand in their defense, come to the podium, and explain their actions to the church." He looked directly from Roy Wallace to Charlie Miller and Steve Hanson and waited. Walter Tate was not present.

To everyone's surprise, it was Steve Hanson who stood and came forward among the din of the Masons' complaints, not Roy Wallace. He stood at the pulpit until the church fell silent again. "I guess there has always been one thing I have held onto all my life, and that's my integrity. I have prepared the prescriptions for almost every one of you for years in my pharmacy. You have trusted me. You showed that trust when you called me to serve on the board of this church."

Steve stopped and drew a deep breath. "Before this congregation and before God, I have to confess that I violated that trust at the board meeting this week when we fired Jeff Moore. We met in secret at the Lodge in advance of the meeting and predetermined its outcome, knowing we held the majority." There was now total silence in the congregation.

He looked directly at Roy Wallace. "We used our office in the church to benefit the Lodge, not to serve the interests of this church. We did so with full understanding of what we were doing. The only honest voice in that meeting was the voice of Win Johnson."

Steve turned and faced Jeff. "I know I have sinned in what I did to you, Jeff, and I can only ask your forgiveness and that of your wife." He turned and spoke to Sue Johnson. "Sue, I sat there in the Lodge while everyone talked about making an example of

Win. I swear I had no idea we would burn him out and put him in the hospital. I take equal responsibility with every Mason in this room for that crime. I am so very sorry. Please forgive me."

He looked down at Jennifer, sitting next to Sue. "Jenny, I feel so bad about your little dog. It was such a deliberate, vicious thing meant only to hurt you. Please believe me when I tell you I had no part in that despicable act."

Tears streamed down his face as he addressed the crowd once again. "I hereby formally announce my resignation from the Masonic Order. I placed the formal demit letter in yesterday's mail, so that you would know I had taken that action before this meeting. I am so ashamed of my involvement in these deeds of darkness and call on every Mason who claims to be a Christian to do likewise. God help us," he sobbed as he turned from the pulpit.

Mick returned to the pulpit. "Do either of the other men have something to say?" he asked.

Roy Wallace stood and spoke sharply to the congregation. "I don't have anything to say to this crowd, except goodbye and good riddance. Any Mason who is a real man will walk out the door with me. I'll take the Lodge over a church like this any day! You can have my membership!" With those words, he worked his way to the aisle and out the door, among the dozens of Masons leaving with him. Charlie Miller stood silently and left without a word.

As the church quieted down again, Jeff smiled as Tom Adams stood and nervously laughed. "Well, I guess a few of us *Masons* are still here. I joined the

Lodge because it was supposed to be a place of fun and fellowship. Win Johnson is my good friend. When his place was burned, I wouldn't believe my brothers in the Lodge could have ever been part of that. I know better today. I guess I'll be looking for a job tomorrow when Charlie finds out I stayed. But I read the stuff you left at my house. That Christian Proclamation on Freemasonry did it for me! I don't belong there in that stuff. I just pray that God and all you people forgive me."

Jeff stepped up to the microphone. "Tom, Steve, and the rest of you men, we love you and forgive you. We are so grateful that you shared how the Lord has changed you today. Look around you at the peace that has come into all this turmoil. Your broken hearts have opened the door for the Holy Spirit to work among us. In just a few minutes Mick is going to finish that discussion and vote on the board issue. Then I'm going to go over that Proclamation with the whole congregation and we're going to vote on incorporating it into our bylaws to prevent something like this from ever happening here again. But right now I think the Holy Spirit has other work to do among us."

Jeff looked out among the congregation and saw a number of faces he recognized from the Lodge. He also saw Tiny sitting in the back watching him with great intent. "I have to believe there are a number of us here today who really need a fresh start. If the Lord has touched your life today, if you want to declare to Him that you have put those *hidden things of darkness* behind you and want to place your trust and your life in Christ, I want you to stand among your church family here today and let me pray with you."

Jeff waited as men and women began to stand throughout the church. He turned and smiled at Mick, who was weeping openly now in joyous victory as God restored their church. Way in the back of the church, Tiny stood with the rest, his eyes locking for a moment on Jeff's.

Why do I ever doubt the power of God? Jeff thought. Out of the ashes of an old hardware store came this gift of a soul set free. That *something really good* that Tiny had promised the other morning was standing there asking Jesus into his heart.

Jeff looked at his grinning wife, who was hugging Sue Johnson. God is going to heal this thing with her mom and dad, he thought. He isn't finished with the folks in Badger Lake yet.

PROCLAMATION

To the Christian Churches
Regarding the Participation of Christians
in Freemasonry

Whereas, Freemasonry declares that its Deity, the "Great Architect of the Universe," can be worshiped by all men, whether they be Buddhists, Christians, Muslims, or Hindus, without controversy,[1] while the Bible teaches that only through Jesus Christ can God be worshiped (John 14:6; 1 Timothy 2:5; 1 John 2:22,23); and

Whereas, Freemasonry refuses to acknowledge the unique Godhood of Jesus Christ[2] or that He died for our sins[3] and rose from the dead,[4] while the Bible teaches that Jesus Christ is truly God Almighty come in the flesh, who died for our sins and rose again (John 1:1-14; Colossians 1:15; 2:9; 1 Corinthians 15:4); and

Whereas, Freemasonry denies the unique and inerrant character of the Holy Bible as the Word of God by saying that it is no better or worse than any other holy book,[5] while the Bible teaches of itself that it is truly the inspired Word of God (2 Timothy 3:16; Matthew 5:18; 1 Peter 1:25; Psalm 119:89; 12:6,7; 19:7,8); and

Whereas, Freemasonry declares that man can be saved by his own labors without faith in Jesus' sacrifice on the cross,[6] while the Bible teaches that a person can be saved only by grace, through faith in Christ (Romans 10:9,10; Ephesians 2:8,9); and

Whereas, Freemasonry blasphemes the name of God by associating it with pagan fertility gods such as Baal,[7] while the Bible affirms the absolute holiness, separateness, and majesty of God's name (Exodus 20:2-7; Deuteronomy 6:4,5; Psalm 8:1; 29:2); and

Whereas, Freemasonry refuses to warn its members about the dangers of an everlasting hell,[8] while the Bible is insistent and urgent in its warnings concerning the dangers of damnation (Matthew 13:49,50; 25:31-46; 2 Thessalonians 1:7-9); and

Whereas, Freemasonry requires that men swear oaths on a Bible in the name of God involving mutilation and murder of human beings,[9] while the New Testament forbids the taking of oaths (Matthew 5:34-37; James 5:12) and the Bible forbids taking God's name in vain and committing murder (Exodus 20:7,13); and

Whereas, Freemasonry links its members in solemn, spiritual bondage to one another, irrespective of members' creeds,[10] while the Bible forbids Christians from being unequally yoked with unbelievers (2 Corinthians 6:14-17; Revelation 18:1-4); and

Whereas, Freemasonry forbids a Christian Mason from witnessing Jesus Christ to his fellow lodge members who are unsaved,[11] while Jesus Himself commands His church to preach the gospel to everyone (Matthew 28:19; Mark 16:15); and

Whereas, Freemasonry aims at the improvement of the natural man only (1 Corinthians 2:14; Colossians 2:8), thus incorrectly channeling by bad interpretation vital spiritual terms (2 Peter 3:16); and

Whereas, Freemasonry insists on keeping its supposedly valuable truths bound under the most serious of secret oaths and available only to a very few, while the Bible does not allow for such secrecy (Matthew 10:26,27; John 18:20; Acts 26:26); and

Whereas, Freemasonry demands that its members call its leaders titles like "Worshipful Master," and kneel before them[12] while the Bible commands us to call no one master save Jesus (Matthew 6:24; 23:8-10) and to worship none save God (Matthew 4:10; Acts 10:25,26; Revelation 22:8,9); and

Whereas, Freemasonry absorbs the loyalties (Luke 9:62), time (Ephesians 5:16), and emotional and spiritual resources and finances of Christian Masons away from the God-ordained tasks of the church, such as overseas missions, evangelism, and taking care of the poor to the glory of Jesus' name (Matthew 6:1-3; 28:19,20; Luke 6:38; James 1:27);

Therefore, we, as humble servants of Jesus Christ and ministers of His gospel, call upon all pastors and Christian leaders of all denominations to take a firm stand in their preaching against the cult of Freemasonry—a rival religion to Christianity which has too long been winked at, tolerated, or even praised by Christian churches. "How long halt ye between two opinions? If the Lord be God, follow him; but if Baal, then follow him"—1 Kings 18:21.

---

1. Albert Pike, 33°, *Morals and Dogma of the Ancient and Accepted Scottish Rite of Freemasonry,* 1966, p. 226; and Albert Mackey, 33°, *Mackey's Revised Encyclopedia of Freemasonry,* (1966), pp. 8-9.

2. Ibid., p. 525; also see Henry Clausen, 33°, *Practice and Procedure for the Scottish Rite,* (1981), pp. 75-77; R.S. Clymer, *The Mysticism of Masonry,* (1900), p. 47; and J.D. Buck, *Symbolism of Mystic Masonry,* (1925), p. 57.

3. Manly P. Hall, 33°, *The Lost Keys of Freemasonry* (1976), pp. 90-91.

4. Pike, *Morals,* p. 539.

5. *Mackey's Revised Encyclopedia of Freemasonry,* (1966), p. 133; also Henry W. Coil, *Coil's Masonic Encyclopedia* (1961), p. 520; and Oliver Day Street, *Symbolism of the Three Degrees* (1924), pp. 44-45.

6. Simmons and Macoy, *Standard Masonic Monitor of the Degrees of Entered Apprentice, Fellowcraft and Master Mason* (1984), pp. 111, 125; also C.H. Lacquement, "Freemasonry and Organized Religions," in *The Pennsylvania Freemason,* Feb. (1989), p. 7.

7. Malcolm C. Duncan, *Duncan's Masonic Ritual and Monitor,* (1974), pp. 224-25, 250-51.

8. *Masonic Monitor of the Degrees of Entered Apprentice, Fellowcraft and Master Mason* (Arkansas: F. & A.M., 1983), p. 15.

9. Duncan, *Ritual*, pp. 35, 65, 96.

10. Ibid., p. 36.

11. Pike, *Morals*, p. 167; Mackey, *Encyclopedia*, 1:192; and J. Blanchard, *Scottish Rite Masonry Illustrated*, (1979), 2:47.

12. Duncan, *Ritual*, p. 13.

Other Good
Harvest House Reading

WHAT YOU NEED TO KNOW ABOUT MORMONS
by *Ed Decker*

In this informative book, the differences between Mormonism and Christianity are clearly presented through a series of conversations between neighbors, which sheds light on the basic tenets of Mormonism and the countering truths of the Bible.

WHAT YOU NEED TO KNOW ABOUT JEHOVAH'S WITNESSES
by *Lorri MacGregor*

One day in his devoted work for the Watch Tower Society, Joe Simpson finds himself on the doorstep of a concerned Christian who has learned how to talk to Jehovah's Witnesses. In the resulting conversation, the key elements of Jehovah's Witness doctrine are clearly and memorably refuted with Christian love and Scripture.

CULT WATCH
by *John Ankerberg* and *John Weldon*

Cult Watch provides historical background and the vital facts on the major beliefs of modern religious movements and looks closely at the reasons people become entrapped in them. Drawing from years of research and interaction with representatives of each movement, the authors offer penetrating analysis of how each religious system clearly contrasts with the essential doctrines of biblical Christianity.